The
UNOFFICIAL
HOBBIT
TRIVIA
CHALLENGE

The
UNOFFICIAL
HOBBIT
TRIVIA
CHALLENGE

Test Your Knowledge and Prove You're a Real Fan!

NICK HURWITCH

Avon, Massachusetts

Published by
Adams Media, a division of F+W Media, Inc.
57 Littlefield Street, Avon, MA 02322. U.S.A.
www.adamsmedia.com

ISBN 10: 1-4405-4260-0
ISBN 13: 978-1-4405-4260-2
eISBN 10: 1-4405-4287-2
eISBN 13: 978-1-4405-4287-9

Printed in the United States of America.

10   9   8   7   6   5   4   3   2   1

Library of Congress Cataloging-in-Publication Data
Hurwitch, Nick.
The unofficial Hobbit trivia challenge / Nick Hurwitch.
p. cm.
ISBN 978-1-4405-4260-2 (pbk.) – ISBN 1-4405-4260-0 (pbk.) – ISBN 978-1-4405-4287-9
(ebook) – ISBN 1-4405-4287-2 (ebook)
1. Tolkien, J. R. R. (John Ronald Reuel), 1892–1973–Miscellanea. 2. Tolkien, J. R. R. (John
Ronald Reuel), 1892–1973. Hobbit. 3. Middle Earth (Imaginary place)–Miscellanea. 4. Fantasy
literature, English–Miscellanea. I. Title.
PR6039.O32Z66138 2012
823'.912–dc23
                                    2012026379

This publication is designed to provide accurate and authoritative information with regard to the
subject matter covered. It is sold with the understanding that the publisher is not engaged in ren-
dering legal, accounting, or other professional advice. If legal advice or other expert assistance is
required, the services of a competent professional person should be sought.

—From a *Declaration of Principles* jointly adopted by a Committee of the American Bar
Association and a Committee of Publishers and Associations

Many of the designations used by manufacturers and sellers to distinguish their product are claimed
as trademarks. Where those designations appear in this book and Adams Media was aware of a
trademark claim, the designations have been printed with initial capital letters.

Interior images © 123rf.com.

This book is available at quantity discounts for bulk purchases.
For information, please call 1-800-289-0963.

DEDICATION

To Amanda, the Lúthien to my Beren.

ACKNOWLEDGMENTS

Amanda, who was a light for me in dark places, when all other lights went out. Through the deepest depths of sleepless nights, across the peaks of mountains of research, and through the desolation of deadlines, she was there. My Lúthien, my Arwen, my Rosie.

Peter Archer, for having hobbits on the brain and for leading the charge to the Lonely Mountain—there and back again.

Brandi Bowles, for dealing with my panicked e-mails and recognizing my strengths.

Peter Jackson, for not recognizing limitations.

Victoria Sandbrook, for keeping the trivia ship sailing.

Christopher Tolkien, for recognizing that Middle-earth was too big for just one man.

J.R.R. Tolkien, for creating a world where we even have the pleasure of knowing about the furry-footed folk called "hobbits." Despite having one of the greatest imaginations of the twentieth century, he never shied away from the world within his mind.

And to the army of fans, historians, academics, and researchers who came before me and did a much better job than I ever could: Douglas A. Anderson, Karen Wynn Fonstad, Robert Foster, John D. Rateliff, Tom Shippey, and countless dedicated fans online. This book would not be possible without them.

CONTENTS

The Unofficial Hobbit Trivia Challenge

Somewhere in your life there lives a hobbit.

At least you should hope there is if you have any intention of making it through this book. What you have here is the ultimate test of your Bilbo brains, your Smaug smarts, and your Mirkwood memory. Don't know what I'm talking about? No? Then you're already in peril. Some might even argue that the path before you is more precarious than Bilbo's was all those years ago when Gandalf showed up at his doorstep and pushed him out into the world. You, after all, will have no map, no wizard or dwarf companions, and certainly won't be seeing any eagles swoop in to save you anytime soon.

Yup. Eight hundred questions from now, you'll either be a legend of Middle-earth mastery, or you'll be wishing you had stayed home, drinking tea and eating seed-cake. Things will get serious; things will get difficult; you may even require an elvish sword.

Though it may be hard to imagine now, *The Hobbit* came from humble beginnings. J.R.R. Tolkien was a professor of Middle English, living in the middle of England, well into middle age, when his children's story landed in the hands of a British publisher. And though *The Hobbit* did remarkably well in its own right, nothing could have prepared him for the places Mr. Bilbo Baggins would take him. After the explosion in popularity of *The Lord of the Rings*, the unassuming linguist became a cultural icon, and the little book that started it all has lost nary a step in popularity in the decades since its initial publication.

Tolkien didn't set out to become a world-renowned author, but that's precisely what happened. He spent much of the rest of his life building a universe that would enthrall millions—perhaps billions. Of course, if you have this book in your hands, you probably already know this: You're one of them!

As one of them, perhaps a hobbit, or a dwarf, or an elf at heart, you also know that *The Hobbit* is just the tip of the Tolkien iceberg. Bilbo's tale sets the stage for one of the most complex and detailed fictional worlds ever created. Unique races, challenging languages, trying tales, kick-ass weapons, and a history of fantastic adventures stand between you and immortality. So don your *mithril* mail and leave all else that you can behind. We travel light. Let's hunt some trivia.

how to use this book

Once you've quested your way through the questions, it'll be time to tally up your score. Do you have what it takes to entertain Tolkien himself? Or are you still a newbie in need of some training?

Answer the questions in the quizzes, and check your answers in the key at the end of every chapter. Each answer is worth one point. Matching questions can earn you up to four points if you pair the answers correctly! Tally your points and see how well you did in the chapter scorecard.

Once you've taken all nine quizzes, flip to the Fan Scorecard at the end of the book. Add your scores for each chapter and see if you're worthy to dwell in Middle-earth!

CHAPTER 1

The hobbit himself

"**I**n a hole in the ground there lived a hobbit." These simple words, scribbled by J.R.R. Tolkien on the back of a student's paper, ushered in a vast universe of landscapes, villains, languages, histories, and adventures. And at the center of them all stood the unlikeliest of heroes: a small, furry-footed hobbit.

When famed wizard Gandalf the Grey arrived at Bilbo's quiet doorstep with promises of adventure, burglary, and treasure, Bilbo was quite content to stay put, thank you very much. A hobbit had no need for adventure and was typically quite content to spend his days eating, drinking, smoking, relaxing, and then eating once more. Still, there was a part of Bilbo that was tickled and intrigued by the idea of venturing out into the world; something in his blood that yearned for mountains and elves and perhaps simply for a tale to tell. There was a part of him that was fearful, too, but before he could say "Bracegirdle," he was marching down the road into the unknown, wondering quite how he would manage in the wild without his favorite pipe.

But being unexpected, and a bit unwilling, is precisely what makes Bilbo such a compelling hero, like his nephew after him. He is of no great physical stature, standing less than four feet tall, nor is he of great physical gifts, what with the cakes and pints of mead packed around his middle. He has no training in battle, nor does he have any great claim to riches, fame, or a brand of magic. Yet he is clever, good-hearted, and brave despite himself. He is, after all, a hobbit.

See how much you know about one of the truest heroes of Middle-earth: Mr. Bilbo Baggins.

1. Entire rooms of a hobbit's home are said to be devoted to what?

_____

2. Thorin refers to Bilbo in a number of ways. Which of these is not one of them?

○ **A.** Audacious hobbit

○ **B.** Fellow conspirator

○ **C.** Scourge of the spiders

○ **D.** Descendant of rats

3. Bilbo's coat of _mithril_ was made by the elves.

○ **A.** True.

○ **B.** False.

4. What game was Bilbo's great-great-granduncle, Bullroarer, said to have invented?

_____

5. Bilbo's first attempt at burglary doesn't go so well. Who (or what) catches him?

_____

SAY "UNCLE"

In The Lord of the Rings, Bilbo refers to Frodo as his "nephew." Naturally, this implies that one of Frodo's parents should be Bilbo's brother or sister. Bilbo, however, is in fact an only child. His parents and Frodo's grandparents were cousins; their fathers, brothers. This means that Bilbo and Frodo's parents are second cousins, which makes Bilbo and Frodo second cousins once removed. Got it? Still, "uncle" is often used as a term of endearment for close elder family members and friends. After all, "My dear Second-Cousin-Once-Removed Bilbo," would have been quite the mouthful.

6. When Bilbo awoke, he first found the ring because it was the only thing he could see inside the pitch-black goblin's cave.

    ○ **A.** True.

    ○ **B.** False.

7. Unlike most hobbits, Bilbo spent his youth learning how to swim in the Shire's lakes with his great paddle-like feet.

    ○ **A.** True.

    ○ **B.** False.

8. With all the food they can pack away, hobbits have a good deal of intestinal fortitude. Which of the following, however, makes Bilbo queasy?

    ○ **A.** Heights

    ○ **B.** Raw fish

    ○ **C.** Barrel-riding

    ○ **D.** Running

WhAT DO hObBiTS EAT?

Tolkien remarked on several occasions that he was similar to a hobbit, not the least because he liked "good, plain food." Bilbo certainly keeps a full larder of the kinds of things one would expect to find in an English kitchen in the 1920s and 1930s: tea cakes, seed-cakes, buttered scones, jam, tarts, mincepies, cheese, pork-pies, and salad. From all this (and remembering that Bilbo was a bachelor), we can form an idea of hobbits' appetites.

Once on the road, the fare is considerably poorer, though if the meal Frodo and his friends have at the Prancing Pony in Bree is any indication, the inns between Hobbiton and Rivendell still keep a good table. The Pony serves the hobbits "hot soup, cold meats, a blackberry tart, new loaves, slabs of butter, and half a ripe cheese." Once they enter the wild, though, Bilbo and the dwarves are on leaner rations, mostly cram. (Frodo and company, being somewhat luckier, get lembas, which is much tastier than cram.)

At Beorn's hall, the hobbit gets fatter on honey, clotted cream, and bread, so it's not until he reaches Lake-town that his diet goes back to something normal.

As a broad generalization, we can say that elves are vegetarians (there's no mention of meat being served at any elven feasts), while dwarves eat meat and drink beer, and hobbits eat anything in sight that isn't nailed to the table.

9. Bilbo spent much of his childhood at "quoits, dart-throwing, shooting at the wand, bowls, ninepins" and other games. What skill did this help Bilbo develop that came in handy during his battle with giant spiders?

_____

10. Bilbo escapes from the Wood-elves' cave inside an empty wine barrel.

○ **A.** True.

○ **B.** False.

hobbit-in-boots

One of the defining characteristics of Bilbo and his fellow hobbits are their large, furry feet, which go uncovered on all terrain and in all weather. However, in an illustration included in the original edition of the book, Bilbo is depicted wearing boots before Smaug and his mound of treasure! In a 1938 letter to his American publisher, Tolkien says, "There is in the text no mention of his acquiring of boots. There should be! It has dropped out somehow or other in the various revisions—the bootings occurred at Rivendell; and he was again bootless after leaving Rivendell on the way home." How one detail can change the way we imagine hobbits!

11. What did Bilbo catch on his ride down the river from Mirkwood to Lake-town?

_____

12. Which of these is not a turn of phrase used by Bilbo's father?

○ **A.** "A hobbit's luck is never up."

○ **B.** "Third time pays for all."

○ **C.** "Every worm has his weak spot."

○ **D.** "While there's life there's hope."

13. The first time Bilbo "burgles" Smaug's hoard, he takes a great red gem.

○ **A.** True.

○ **B.** False.

14. Bilbo's *mithril* mail is hobbit-sized for a reason. For whom had it originally been made?

_____

15. Though quite different from a hobbit's songs, Bilbo found the dwarf songs quite captivating. What feeling overcomes him as he listens to them?

_____

16. Bilbo's adventure is certainly the longest he is ever away from home until he leaves the Shire for good in *The Fellowship of the Ring*. How long is his Unexpected Journey?

_____

17. Fill in the blank: Bilbo considers naming the written account of his adventure "There and Back Again: _____ "

18. Upon his return, Bilbo finds which firm busy auctioning off all his possessions?

_____

19. Bilbo inherited his adventurous spirit from his mother's side of his family. What is Bilbo's mother's maiden name?

_____

20. What animal sounds does Thorin advise Bilbo to mimic if he is in danger?

- ○ **A.** Wolf howls
- ○ **B.** Sparrow chirps
- ○ **C.** Hobbit screams
- ○ **D.** Owl hoots

21. When is Bilbo Baggins's birthday?

_____

22. At the start of his adventure, Bilbo is considered a hobbit of middle age. How old is he then?

_____

23. To which animal is Bilbo most frequently compared (on a total of five separate occasions) in _The Hobbit_?

_____

24. Bilbo's grandfather was famously known as "Old Took." What was Old Took's first name?

_____

25. Bilbo lived longer than any known hobbit; even longer than his grandfather, Old Took.

○ **A.** True.

○ **B.** False.

26. Bilbo was married briefly once, to Primula Underhill of Hobbiton.

○ **A.** True.

○ **B.** False.

27. What were the names of Frodo's parents, Bilbo's cousin and cousin-in-law?

_____

28. Match the film to the actor who played Bilbo Baggins in it.

A. *The Hobbit* (animated)   **i.** Martin Freeman

B. *The Hobbit* (2012–2014)   **ii.** Ian Holm

C. *The Lord of the Rings* (animated)   **iii.** Orson Bean

D. *The Lord of the Rings* (2001–2003) **iv.** Norman Bird

hobbit defined

Having been a man who had worked with dictionaries, and facing many questions about the origin and use of the word "hobbit," Tolkien offered up this definition in 1970 to Robert Burchfield, who was senior editor of the Oxford English Dictionary *at the time: "One of an imaginary people, a small variety of the human race, that gave themselves this name (meaning 'hole-dweller') but were called by others* halflings, *since they were half the height of normal Men."*

29. Fill in the blank: Some adventurers prefer the title "Expert _____" to "burglar."

30. Though they speak in the Common tongue Westron, hobbits have their own provincial dialect, which borrows from the language of Dunland. What is this dialect called?

_____

31. What is the name of Bilbo's cousin, son of Lobelia Bracegirdle and Otho Sackville-Baggins, who seized control of the Shire during the War of the Ring and called himself "The Chief"?

_____

32. What is the word for "hobbit" in the dialect of the hobbits of the Shire (also the Westron word for "hobbit")?

_____

33. "Bilbo" is an Old English term meaning "short sword or rapier."

○ **A.** True.

○ **B.** False.

34. What was the first great hobbit family dynasty, "one of the oldest in the Marish, or indeed in the Shire"?

_____

35. Bilbo's agreement with the dwarves includes one-fourteenth share of all profits, transportation of his earnings, and funeral arrangements, if necessary.

○ **A.** True.

○ **B.** False.

36. Throughout their adventure, several dwarves carry the smaller Bilbo on their backs. Which dwarf never does?

○ **A.** Dori

○ **B.** Nori

○ **C.** Bombur

○ **D.** Balin

37. While on their adventure, what key event occurs on Bilbo's birthday?

_____

hoBBITS, The mISSING LINK

In 2003, the bones of a previously undiscovered species were found on the island of Flores in Indonesia. The Homo floresiensis, *which has been nicknamed "the hobbit," are about three and a half feet tall and share a number of characteristics with both apes and modern man's ancient ancestors,* Homo erectus *(though with a brain about half the size).*

38. What was the name of Bilbo's next-door neighbor at Bag End?

_____

39. Prior to returning to the Shire with his share of the treasure, Bilbo and all the Bagginses were hard-working but generally poor hobbits.

○ **A.** True.

○ **B.** False.

40. What is Bilbo's father's name?

_____

41. Bilbo inherited Bag End from his father, who built it.

○ **A.** True.

○ **B.** False.

42. Accompanied by three dwarves, Bilbo returns to Dale one last time after leaving the Shire, before settling in Rivendell to write his book.

○ **A.** True.

○ **B.** False.

43. As an elderly hobbit, Bilbo boards an elvish ship to leave Middle-earth along with Gandalf and Frodo. Where are they headed?

_____

44. What is the name of the song that Bilbo writes for Aragorn after the Ranger tells the hobbit his history?

_____

45. Bilbo, like Tolkien, was quite the linguist, speaking and studying several languages. What set of translations is considered Bilbo's primary scholarly contribution to Middle-earth?

_____

46. The blood of what type of hobbit is thought to have contributed to Bilbo's love of elves, adventure, and languages? (Hint: It's the least common strain of all hobbits.)

_____

The BOURGEOIS BURGLAR

Several critics, most notably Tom Shippey, have commented on the degree to which Bilbo stands out by reason of his ordinariness (Shippey refers to him as a "bourgeois burglar"). When all the kings and captains are preoccupied with the siege of the Lonely Mountain and the forthcoming battle between the elves and the dwarves, it is Bilbo who brings everything down to Middle-earth. "Personally, I am tired of the whole affair. I wish I was back in the West in my own home, where folk are more reasonable." It's a moment of sanity amid all the epic madness.

Gandalf reinforces this at the end of the story, telling Bilbo, "you are only quite a little fellow in a wide world after all," and Bilbo agrees, laughing.

But of course, that isn't the end of it. Bilbo becomes more and more "elvish," wandering off on long rambles, during which he sees elves. And in the end, he goes first to Rivendell and then into the Utter West to Valinor. Frodo follows a similar course, starting as an ordinary hobbit and then becoming more ethereal and elvish before he leaves the Shire for good.

In the end it's Sam who's the most ordinary and who remains the most "bourgeois"—with his comment at the very end of the saga.

"Well," he says, "I'm back."

47. What well-known character from *The Lord of the Rings* named his tenth child after Bilbo?

_____

48. The surname *Took* is an Anglicization of *Tûk*, which means "daring" in the Shire dialect.

○ **A.** True.

○ **B.** False.

BILBO BAGGINS DRAGON SLAYER

In the original manuscript of The Hobbit, *and for the first several drafts, Bilbo took a more active role in slaying Smaug. Indeed, Bilbo smote the dragon twice—once with his knife and once with a spear found in the halls under the mountain amongst the treasure. Ultimately, though, Tolkien found this too implausible and worried that it would have a negative effect on Bilbo's character. Bilbo Baggins was many things, but a sneaky murderer of dragons was not one of them.*

49. Baggins is an anglicized translation of a hobbit surname. What is the name for "Baggins" in the Shire dialect of Westron?

_____

50. In the dialect of the hobbits of the Shire, names ending with an "a" are considered masculine.

○ **A.** True.

○ **B.** False.

51. Bilbo taught Frodo the elvish language Quenya, a fact later remarked on by the elf Gildor.

○ **A.** True.

○ **B.** False.

52. Bilbo was only nine years old when his grandfather, Old Took, died of old age. How old was his grandfather when he died?

_____

53. Bilbo wears the ring several times in his adventure to the Lonely Mountain, and presumably many more times before giving it to Frodo. When does he put it on for the last time?

---

54. In *Unfinished Tales*, Gandalf claimed that he chose Bilbo for the journey to "educate" the dwarves about Shirelings.

- ○ **A.** True.
- ○ **B.** False.

55. The Shire dialect of the language Westron was adopted from the men of Anduin, and therefore suggests a close relationship between the Big Folk and Little Folk prior to the hobbits' migration to the Shire.

- ○ **A.** True.
- ○ **B.** False.

56. What is the name of the poem Tolkien wrote about Bilbo and the last journey to the Grey Havens?

---

57. The poem mentioned in Question 56 was illustrated as a poster, a reproduction of which later appeared in a book. Who was the artist?

---

58. What event does Bilbo consider to be the worst experience of his life?

_____

59. When he arrives at Bag End, Balin requests a very specific kind of cake from Bilbo. What kind of cake does he ask for?

_____

60. In _The Fellowship of the Ring_, Bilbo gives his _mithril_ coat of mail to Frodo. Where in the Shire was the mail kept before Bilbo took it to Rivendell?

_____

61. What is the only type of hobbit that can grow a beard?

_____

GOLLUM'S REVENGE

Motivated by the loss of his precious, Gollum left the lake under the Misty Mountains. But he was captured in Mordor and tortured for information. It was from Gollum that Sauron learned of the halflings and sent his Ringwraiths in pursuit of the ring. However, he also set Gollum free, sensing his hatred for the hobbit who had robbed him, believing there was a chance that Gollum would exact his revenge and help Sauron to the ring. His plan, of course, did not pan out, but Gollum did what he could to make life difficult for Bilbo's heir.

62. Fill in the blank: Though Bilbo and the dwarves both lived underground, the hobbit generally had a better sense of _____ than the dwarves.

63. At various points in his adventure, Bilbo wishes he was back in his hobbit-hole with the kettle on the hob just beginning to sing. Which of these is *not* a traditional meaning of the word "hob"?

○ **A.** Imaginary being

○ **B.** A sweet drink

○ **C.** Fairy

○ **D.** Elf

64. In order to prevent the dwarves from going to war with the men of Dale and the Wood-elves, what stolen item does Bilbo use as a bargaining chip?

_____

65. Prior to leaving with Gandalf and the dwarves, Bilbo was well-liked and respected in the Shire.

○ **A.** True.

○ **B.** False.

66. Upon establishing the Shire, the hobbits began their own calendar beginning at Year Zero.

○ **A.** True.

○ **B.** False.

67. What word did hobbits use to refer to anything they had no immediate use for but could not bring themselves to throw away?

_____

68. What three important relics of his adventure with Thorin's party does Bilbo take with him when he leaves Bag End for good?

_____

69. What nickname did Bilbo earn in the Shire later in life, earned after vanishing on his eleventy-first birthday?

_____

70. The name "Bilbo" is in fact an existing surname in England and America—and was even the name of a Mississippi senator in the first half of the twentieth century.

○ **A.** True.

○ **B.** False.

71. Tolkien himself created a hand-drawn, hand-written facsimile of Bilbo's contract with the dwarves.

○ **A.** True.

○ **B.** False.

BILBO BAGGINS, POET

More than most hobbits, Bilbo was quite scholarly. He is credited with writing several songs and poems, as well as historical and linguistic books, much like Tolkien himself. In fact, Bilbo was in many ways an extension of Tolkien in the history of Middle-earth. Most poems and sources that would have otherwise been attributed to an omniscient narrator were instead attributed to Bilbo. Although hobbits kept detailed histories of family trees, and were known for their songs and merrymaking, scholarly pursuits and authorship among halflings were quite unusual before Bilbo Baggins.

72. The original *Red Book of Westmarch* contained a full and accurate account of Bilbo's encounter with Gollum.

○ **A.** True.

○ **B.** False.

73. Bilbo and Frodo are both around fifty years of age when they leave the Shire on their respective journeys. At what age are hobbits considered adults?

_____

74. As recounted in *The Quest of Erebor*, when Gandalf came in search of Bilbo for Thorin's party, the wizard turned to this hobbit to learn his whereabouts. (Hint: A young Hamfast Gamgee was apprenticed to the hobbit in question.)

_____

75. Despite his attachment to the ring, Bilbo was present at the Council of Elrond when the decision was made to destroy it.

  ○ **A.** True.

  ○ **B.** False.

76. How many years pass between the end of Bilbo's journey and the start of Frodo's in *The Lord of the Rings*?

  ○ **A.** Fifty-nine years and three months exactly

  ○ **B.** Approximately 100 years

  ○ **C.** Forty-two and a half years

  ○ **D.** Less than thirty years

77. Prior to being "recruited" by Gandalf, Bilbo was known to wander off for days at a time without telling any hobbits where he was going.

  ○ **A.** True.

  ○ **B.** False.

78. When Balin first arrives at Bilbo's doorstep, it's the first time the hobbit ever meets or speaks to a dwarf.

  ○ **A.** True.

  ○ **B.** False.

79. Of Bilbo's many poems, which one appears in various incarnations three different times in *The Lord of the Rings*?

80. After retiring to Rivendell, Bilbo spends much of his time writing poetry. At the banquet honoring Frodo and his friends after their arrival, Bilbo recites one long poem to an admiring audience of elves. Who is the subject of the poem?

_____

81. Though he was blind to the origins of the ring for many years, something about Bilbo finally makes Gandalf suspicious of it. What does he notice?

_____

82. Bilbo's mother was the ninth child born to her mother, Adamanta, and father, Gerontius. How many siblings did she have?

_____

83. What two pieces of information (indeed, what two words) did Bilbo let slip to Gollum during their riddle game, words later tortured out of Gollum in Mordor?

_____

84. Who possessed the One Ring before Gollum (the same man who defeated Sauron and was Aragorn's ancestor)?

_____

BILBO'S LAST SONG

The poem written by Tolkien about Bilbo, on the shores of Middle-earth about to depart Middle-earth on a ship to the Grey Havens, traveled about as long a road as its subject. The poem was originally titled "Vestr um haf" and had no connection to Bilbo. Tolkien altered the title—and the text—in October 1968. He then gave the poem to his secretary, Joy Hill, as a gift when she discovered it in his office. It was once set to music and later illustrated as a poster, but wasn't published in a book until 1990. The poem is in first person, sung by Bilbo.

85. What is the name of the book Bilbo writes late in life, the book that is the "source" of Tolkien's tales?

_____

86. What did Bilbo do with the gold he and Gandalf recovered from its hiding place near the stone trolls at the end of *The Hobbit*?

_____

87. Match the type of hobbit to their defining attributes.

A. Stoors   i. Larger, with a heavier build

B. Harfoots   ii. Medium-sized

C. Fallohides   iii. Fair-haired and fair-skinned

88. Fallohide hobbits are credited with holding longest to the hobbit tradition of living underground.

○ A. True

○ B. False

89. Which of these was not mentioned as something that Bilbo usually took with him when leaving home?

○ **A.** Pipe

○ **B.** Pocket-handkerchief

○ **C.** Walking-stick

○ **D.** Hat

90. Bilbo's shirt has diamond-studded buttons that only come unclasped when ordered, a gift from his late grandfather.

○ **A.** True.

○ **B.** False.

91. What was Tolkien's original title for Bilbo's poem, "The Road Goes Ever On"?

_____

The shire's most eligible bachelor

For all of their similarities, there was one area in which Bilbo was markedly different from his creator: his love life. Bilbo was a lifelong bachelor. This is especially surprising given Tolkien's devotion to his wife, Edith, and their four children. It is speculated that Bilbo's mysterious adventure marred his image as a good potential husband. It could also be that the ring changed Bilbo and pulled him from society, as it did Gollum. Even so, judging by the age of halfling children, hobbits typically married in their forties. Bilbo was over fifty when he left on his adventure. Frodo, like his uncle, remained a bachelor.

92. Bilbo tells Smaug that the hobbit was "chosen" for a particular reason, inadvertently revealing that he is not alone. What is the reason?

_____

93. In the preface to _The Lord of the Rings_, Tolkien makes a reference to a strong Fallohide strain that could be found among some families of hobbits, particularly the Tooks. Among which hobbits was there a strong strain traceable to the Stoors?

_____

94. Bilbo's father's family, though large, was considerably smaller than Bilbo's mother's. How many aunts and uncles did Bilbo have on his father's side?

_____

95. After returning home, where did Bilbo keep Sting?

_____

Chapter 1 Answer Key

1.	Clothing.	25.	True.
2.	C.	26.	False. Bilbo was a lifelong bachelor.
3.	False. It was made by dwarves.	27.	Drogo and Primula.
4.	Golf.	28.	A-iii, B-i, C-iv, D-ii.
5.	A talking purse.	29.	Treasure hunter.
6.	False. He felt the ring with his hand.	30.	Hobbitish.
7.	False. Bilbo could not swim.	31.	Lotho Sackville-Baggins.
8.	A.	32.	Kuduk.
9.	Stone throwing.	33.	True.
10.	False. He had to grab onto a barrel while wearing the ring. He was not inside a barrel.	34.	The Oldbucks.
11.	A cold.	35.	False. It does not include the transportation of earnings, a point of contention later in the book.
12.	A.	36.	B.
13.	False. He takes a two-handled cup.	37.	The party arrives by barrel at Lake-town.
14.	A young elf prince.	38.	Gaffer Gamgee.
15.	A love of beautiful things.	39.	False. They were among the wealthiest families in the Shire.
16.	Fourteen months.	40.	Bungo Baggins.
17.	A Hobbit's Journey.	41.	True.
18.	Grubb, Grubb, and Burrowes.	42.	True.
19.	Belladonna Took.	43.	The Undying Lands.
20.	D.	44.	"All that is gold does not glitter."
21.	September 22.	45.	Three volumes of lore, labeled Translations from the Elvish, by B. B.
22.	Fifty-one.	46.	Fallohide.
23.	A rabbit.	47.	Samwise Gamgee.
24.	Gerontius.		

48.	True.		72.	False. It contained the account wherein Gollum promised Bilbo the ring as a present if he won the riddle game.
49.	Labingi.			
50.	True. The "o" we recognize at the end of male Hobbits' names are the result of English translation, according to Tolkien.		73.	Thirty-three.
			74.	Holman Greenhand (Holman the gardener).
51.	True. "Be careful, friends," says the elf. "Here is a scholar in the Ancient Tongue. Bilbo was a good master."		75.	True.
			76.	A.
52.	130.		77.	True.
53.	At his 111th birthday party (The Farewell Party).		78.	False.
54.	True.		79.	"The Road Goes Ever On."
55.	True.		80.	Eärendil the mariner.
56.	Bilbo's Last Song.		81.	Bilbo is very slow to age.
57.	Pauline Baynes.		82.	Eleven.
58.	The Battle of Five Armies.		83.	"Shire" and "Baggins."
59.	Seed-cake.		84.	Isildur.
60.	Michel Delving Museum.		85.	The Red Book of Westmarch.
61.	Stoors, many of whom have down on their chins.		86.	He gave it away, since it came from thieves and he didn't believe it was rightfully his.
62.	Sight.			
63.	B.		87.	A-i, B-ii, C-iii.
64.	The Arkenstone.		88.	False. This is true of the Harfoots.
65.	True.		89.	A.
66.	False. They began at Year One.		90.	False. Bilbo's buttons are brass.
67.	Mathom.		91.	"The Road Goes Ever Ever On."
68.	His *mithril* coat, Sting, and his old cloak and hood, given to him by Dwalin.		92.	For his "lucky number."
69.	Mad Baggins.		93.	The Brandybucks.
70.	True.		94.	Four.
71.	True.		95.	Over the mantelpiece.

Score Your Hobbit Know-How!

In this section, there are 100 possible right answers.

If you got 0–34 right, you must be a Sackville-Baggins: wanting all of the reward with none of the hard work!

If you got 35–65 right, you're a Bracegirdle from Hardbottle. You might not be the brightest hobbit in the Shire, but at least you're invited to all of the happening parties.

If you got 66–100 right, a sincere congrats is in order. With your Tookish blood, you might just be ready for your next great adventure.

FRIENDS AND ALLIES

Though their adventures and riddles are at the core of Tolkien's tales, hobbits are but one of many races that dwell in Middle-earth. At that, they are historically a minor and secluded kind, more apt to take a blade to a wheel of cheese than to an enemy. Indeed, had Gandalf never appeared on Bilbo's doorstep and coaxed him from his hobbit-hole, the world might never have heard of hobbits at all.

Yet, despite the prevailing skepticism about hobbits' abilities, stemming from their stature and affinity for pipe-weed, hobbits manage to endear themselves to the other good-natured inhabitants of Middle-earth, in large part due to Bilbo and his kin. Wizards, dwarves, elves, and men are but a few of the peoples that befriend, help, and are in turn helped by the unassuming halflings of the Shire.

Birds of all shapes and sizes, from owls and eagles to crows and thrushes; talking trees, sentient horses, and shape-shifters; all of the creatures of Tolkien's Middle-earth have a place in the world—as well as their own strengths and weaknesses.

Most of Bilbo's party is comprised of dwarves, on a quest to reclaim their once-great Kingdom Under the Mountain. For all their differences, dwarves and hobbits share a fair number of similarities: diminutive in stature, a tendency to be large around the middle, a love for hearty libations and sizable feasts, a feisty temperament, unanticipated bravery, and a preference to live in the cool, damp comforts of the underground. Though hobbits and dwarves bump heads in matters of business, riches, battle, and stealth (indeed, something of which dwarves have little concept), Bilbo finds his friendships and alliances with Thorin's companions to be strong and lasting. So just how strong and everlasting is your memory?

1. Long before arriving on Bilbo's doorstep, Gandalf was close friends with one of Bilbo's relatives. Who was it?

_____

2. Though it is never said how (or if) Beorn mates or reproduces, his son takes his place as the leader of the shape-shifters. What is Beorn's son's name?

_____

3. One of first dwarves on Bilbo's doorstep for "tea time" is also the first to visit him with Gandalf years after their adventure. Who is it?

_____

4. Why was it that Bard could understand the thrush's warning during Smaug's attack?

_____

5. The elves in Peter Jackson's _The Lord of the Rings_ films are tall, beautiful, mystic, and serious. In what way do they differ from those found in _The Hobbit_?

○ **A.** They are taller

○ **B.** They are unskilled with a bow

○ **C.** They sing and dance merrily

○ **D.** They are shorter—of dwarf height

THE MASTER OF THE LAKE: FRIEND OR FOE

Allegiances in Middle-earth are not always clearly drawn. Though the Master of Lake-town allows Thorin and company to rest in his beds and feast in his halls, it is the people of the town who welcome the dwarves with open arms, not the Master himself. He is skeptical of Thorin's claim to the throne of the King Under the Mountain and later blames him for the destruction of Lake-town. When Bard gives the Master a large share of his Lonely Mountain treasure to rebuild the town, he takes it for himself and absconds to the Waste . . . where he dies of starvation. Just deserts. The Master of Lake-town is no dragon, but enemies in Middle-earth come in all shapes and sizes.

6. Two of the dwarves in Thorin's party are brothers, as well as the youngest of the bunch. Who are they?

_____

7. At one point, Gandalf leaves the party to visit his cousin near the southern border of Mirkwood. What is his name?

_____

8. Shape-shifters such as Beorn are often highly sensitive and touchy. What word can be safely used around Beorn?

○ **A.** Skin-changer

○ **B.** Furrier

○ **C.** Tippet

○ **D.** Muff

9. Other than Wood-elves, name two other kinds of elves that descended from the ancient tribes.

_____

10. The Wood-elves love all trees, but oak trees are their favorite.

○ **A.** True.

○ **B.** False.

11. It is said that the Elvenking of Mirkwood has but one weakness. What is it?

○ **A.** Wine and merriment

○ **B.** Silver and white gems

○ **C.** Gold and green gems

○ **D.** Pride

12. The dwarves escape Mirkwood and ride down the river in empty wine barrels.

○ **A.** True.

○ **B.** False.

13. Once the back door to Smaug's lair has been opened, only one dwarf volunteers to go inside the Lonely Mountain with Bilbo. Who is it?

_____

The Tiptoeing Bear

Beorn loans Bilbo and the dwarves his ponies to reach Mirkwood but fully intends for them to be returned unharmed. Though the dwarves never notice, Bilbo believes he sees the shadow of a bear, Beorn's animal form, behind them and in the distance several times after leaving the Carrock. Whether Beorn holds an interest in their quest or simply wants to protect his ponies is unclear, but he does arrive at the Battle of Five Armies just in time to turn the tide, well after his ponies are safely home.

14. The language of the dwarves was a common tongue, spoken freely from dwarf to dwarf, and from dwarf to man or elf as well.

   ○ **A.** True.

   ○ **B.** False.

15. Bard the Bowman of Lake-town was a descendant of Girion, the Lord of Dale.

   ○ **A.** True.

   ○ **B.** False.

16. Gandalf's name is Norse for "wizard," or, literally, "sorcerer-elf."

   ○ **A.** True.

   ○ **B.** False.

17. Thorin's people had a long relationship with the ravens of the mountain. What was the great raven's name?

_____

tbe mithril mail

Although Bilbo doesn't take his full share of treasure from the Lonely Mountain, his gift from Thorin may be among the most valuable items from the haul. Not only does the mithril mail have value in gold, but it becomes vital to Frodo, to whom Bilbo hands it over. It saves Frodo's life on three separate occasions: when he is stabbed by an orc in Khazad-dûm, when it causes a fight between orcs after Frodo is captured at Cirith Ungol, and when Saruman tries to kill the hobbit upon his return to the Shire.

18. Having left his hobbit-hole in a rush, Bilbo joined the dwarves in a rather unprepared state. Which dwarf gives Bilbo his dark green cloak and hood for the journey?

_____

19. Each member of Dain's army is equipped with a short broadsword and a mail of *mithril*.

○ **A.** True.

○ **B.** False.

20. Which army is the first to charge in the Battle of Five Armies?

_____

21. What item does the Elvenking place upon Thorin's tomb at the end of the Battle of Five Armies?

_____

22. With his share of the treasure under the Mountain, the Master of Lake-town becomes the new King of Dale.

○ **A.** True.

○ **B.** False.

23. The map of the Lonely Mountain changed hands many times. From whom did Gandalf receive it before giving it to Thorin?

ELRONÐ hALF-ELVEN

In The Hobbit we catch a brief glimpse of one of the most powerful characters in Middle-earth: Elrond Half-elven, who lives in Rivendell in the north (also known as Imladris).

Elrond was the product of one of the three elf–human marriages in history, that of Idril and Tuor (the other two being Beren and Lúthien, and Aragorn and Arwen Evenstar). Idril and Tuor gave birth to Eärendil the Mariner, who with his wife Elwing carried the silmaril *into the Uttermost West. Elrond was their son. At the end of the First Age, the Valar gave those of the Half-elven a choice: Would they be elven or mortal? Elrond chose elven-kind, which is why, even though he has mortal blood in his veins, he is generally more elf than human. He was also given the choice of passing into the West from the Grey Havens, and his children were granted the same choice.*

During battles with Sauron in Eregion during the Second Age, Elrond was forced back and eventually found the hidden valley where he created Rivendell.

In The Hobbit, "evil things did not come into that valley," leading one to suppose that Elrond had hedged it round with a good deal of magical protection—hardly surprising when we consider how it was founded.

24. As Bilbo and the dwarves make their way through Mirkwood to the Lonely Mountain, Gandalf is summoned to a great council. What is the name of that council?

_____

25. During the Battle of Five Armies, who kills Bolg and pulls the injured Thorin from the battlefield?

_____

26. Thorin's grandfather, Thrór, first discovers the Lonely Mountain in 1999 of the Third Age.

○ **A.** True.

○ **B.** False.

27. Nearly all of the dwarf names in _The Hobbit_ come from an ancient Norse poem, except for Balin.

○ **A.** True.

○ **B.** False.

28. What is the name of the ancient Norse poem in Question 27?

_____

29. Lord Elrond is one of the oldest inhabitants of Middle-earth. What two races are said to make up his ancestry?

_____

30. Who are the only dwarves in the party not descended from Durin, and are therefore of a different line than Thorin Oakenshield?

_____

31. The Lord of the Eagles in *The Hobbit* is the same eagle who saves Gandalf in *The Lord of the Rings*, Gwaihir the Windlord.

○ **A.** True.

○ **B.** False.

32. As a beekeeper, Beorn makes a number of things out of honey. Fermented honey and water, for example, can be distilled into this delicious libation.

_____

33. Elves are described as being tall, with fair skin and pointy ears.

○ **A.** True.

○ **B.** False.

VÖLUSPÁ, PROPHECY OF SEERESS

Tolkien was deeply interested in Norse poetry and mythology, as is routinely evident in his work. "Völuspá, Prophecy of Seeress" is a famous Nordic poem from the Poetic Etta *(and* Prose Edda, *both famous collections of Old Norse poems) that tells the tale of the creation and impending end of a world. The premise itself has clear parallels to Middle-earth, but Tolkien also used the poem to derive the names of his dwarves, as well as Gandalf. Even the name Oakenshield (*Eikinskialdi*) can be found in the "Völuspá."*

34. In *The Lord of the Rings* we learn the name of the Elvenking, who goes unnamed in *The Hobbit*. What is it?

35. What was Gandalf's name in the original manuscript of *The Hobbit*?

36. Thorin's father also attempted to reclaim the Lonely Mountain using the map before he was killed.

○ **A.** True.

○ **B.** False.

37. Durin was one of the Fathers of the Dwarves. How many Fathers of the Dwarves are there?

38. The elves of Rivendell greet Gandalf, Bilbo, and the dwarves with a great feast.

○ **A.** True.

○ **B.** False.

39. According to *The Quest of Erebor* in *Unfinished Tales*, Gandalf guided Thorin's quest in order to re-establish a strong realm in the north in the event of an attack from southern Mirkwood, where Sauron dwelt.

○ **A.** True.

○ **B.** False.

40. Gandalf was known by the elves as "Tharkûn."

○ **A.** True.

○ **B.** False.

41. The Elvenking is the father of what important character from *The Lord of the Rings* trilogy?

_____

42. Gandalf was a part of an exclusive order sent to Middle-earth by the Valar about 1,000 years into the Third Age. What was the name of that order?

_____

43. The name *Beorn* is an Old English word meaning "man," as well as the Old Norse *björn* meaning what?

_____

The War of the Dwarves and Orcs

Not long before the events of The Hobbit, *a war raged between dwarves and orcs, ignited when Thrór was slain at the hands of Azog in Moria. The dwarves searched for him high and low, ransacking as many orcish lairs as they could find in the Misty Mountains as they went. The remaining forces of orcs finally gathered east of the gates of Moria, and were defeated (along with Azog) at the hands of Durin's Folk. But many dwarves died, and with Moria uninhabitable, Thorin and his father Thráin became wanderers for many years before attempting to re-establish a kingdom in the West.*

44. Only two dwarves in Thorin's party also accompanied Thorin's father, Thráin, on his own journey to the Lonely Mountain. Who were they?

_____

45. Which dwarves of Thorin's party were his nephews, the sons of his sister?

_____

46. About how long are dwarves known to live?

○ **A.** 100 years

○ **B.** 250 years

○ **C.** 500 years

○ **D.** Dwarves are immortal

47. About how long are elves known to live?

    ○ **A.** 100 years

    ○ **B.** 250 years

    ○ **C.** 500 years

    ○ **D.** Elves are immortal

48. What dwarf among the party is the father of Gimli, a member of the Company of the Ring?

_____

49. In Tolkien's original manuscript, Thorin's name was Gandalf.

    ○ **A.** True.

    ○ **B.** False.

50. What gift did Gandalf give Old Took, Bilbo's grandfather on his mother's side?

    ○ **A.** Diamond studs that never came undone unless ordered

    ○ **B.** Parchment and a magic quill

    ○ **C.** An elvish walking stick made of oak

    ○ **D.** A wagon full of fireworks

51. During his council with Saruman at Isengard in the 2001 film *The Fellowship of the Ring*, Gandalf is seen drinking this particular beverage, the same one he orders from Bilbo when he arrives for "tea time."

_____

52. In the live-action *Hobbit* films, Thorin wears nearly all black. But the book describes his stockings as a different color. What shade were they?

_____

53. Bard isn't introduced in *The Hobbit* until Smaug's attack on Lake-town.

○ **A.** True.

○ **B.** False.

54. What feature differentiated Thorin's hood from the hoods of the other dwarves?

○ **A.** He had no hood

○ **B.** It was larger

○ **C.** A golden clasp

○ **D.** A silver tassel

55. Thorin is the king of the dwarves known as "Thráin's Folk."

○ **A.** True.

○ **B.** False.

56. Beorn gives Bilbo and the dwarves new ponies as gifts for burning the orcs and wargs in the forest.

○ **A.** True.

○ **B.** False.

57. Which of the following animals did Beorn *not* keep in his household?

○ **A.** Goats

○ **B.** Sheep

○ **C.** Dogs

○ **D.** Horses

TALKING ANIMALS

The idea of talking animals is almost as old as fairytales themselves. In Tolkien's world, there is a mixture of animals and birds that communicate with humans and others who have anthropomorphic features.

The eagles are the most prominent talking birds. In The Hobbit *Bilbo encounters them when they rescue him, the dwarves, and Gandalf from the goblins and the wargs. The wargs themselves appear to be able to communicate with the goblins, since the two species have planned a joint raid on the woodmen living near the mountains. The eagles appear in* The Lord of the Rings, *most notably in the form of their chief Gwaihir, who speaks easily with Gandalf.*

There are some other species of talking bird in The Hobbit. *The thrush, for instance, tells Bard of Smaug's weakness and attempts to communicate with the dwarves, who aren't able to understand it. ("I cannot follow the speech of such birds, it is very quick and difficult," Balin complains.) Ravens can also speak, and Roäc, their chief, has several extensive conversations with Thorin, which Bilbo is able to follow without difficulty. He has less luck understanding crows, who Balin tells him have been calling him and the dwarves nasty names.*

Beorn, as a shape-changer, can communicate easily with a number of animals—it would appear from Tolkien's description that they each have their own particular language.

Finally, of course, there's Smaug. One wonders what language dragons speak to one another, but Smaug evidently speaks Westron perfectly well— indeed, his conversation with Bilbo sounds like the sort Tolkien might have overheard in the Common Room of Merton College, Oxford.

58. What kind of bird takes the message of Smaug's weakness to Bard the Bowman?

_____

59. What is the name of the dwarves' first song, also featured in the first of *The Hobbit* films?

_____

60. Which dwarf becomes the King Under the Mountain after the Battle of Five Armies?

_____

61. What was Fili and Kili's mother's name?

O **A.** Dain

O **B.** Dís

O **C.** Thráin

O **D.** Dili

62. Despite Gandalf's complaint at the beginning of *The Hobbit* that hobbits generally don't know how to use weapons, fortunately it turns out at the end of *The Lord of the Rings* that they're skilled in the use of what weapon?

_____

tbe five wizaRas

In The Two Towers, Saruman speaks of "the rods of the Five Wizards." These are known as the Istari, who come from Valar. If Saruman and Gandalf are two, and Radagast the Brown is a third, that leaves two wizards unaccounted for. Tolkien has indicated that they likely dwelled to the East (whereas the events of Lord of the Rings *take place in the West). There is one reference to their names in Tolkien's* Unfinished Tales: *They are called "Blue Wizards," named Alatar and Pallano, but are mentioned nowhere else in Tolkien lore.*

63. The dwarves of the Lonely Mountain and the men of Dale regularly fought over territory and resources before Smaug's arrival.

○ **A.** True.

○ **B.** False.

64. In what town did Gandalf and Thorin first meet, when Gandalf first encouraged him to take back his throne in the east?

_____

65. Which dwarf does Thorin consider the strongest member of the party?

_____

66. What is the color of Dain Ironfoot's famed battleaxe?

_____

67. Though it is not explicitly stated in *The Hobbit*, what important character from *The Lord of the Rings*, then ten years old, might Bilbo have met during his first visit to Rivendell?

_____

68. Beorn does not appear in *The Lord of the Rings*, but his kin are referenced several times as guardians of the lands surrounding the Carrock. What are they called?

_____

69. Beorn is a vegetarian.

○ **A.** True.

○ **B.** False.

70. During the War of the Ring, the Elvenking abstains from battles in the East and South, choosing to instead protect his realm in Mirkwood.

○ **A.** True.

○ **B.** False.

71. Who fought with Thorin III Stonehelm to lift a siege on Dale and the Lonely Mountain during the War of the Ring after the death of Dain Ironfoot?

_____

The Lord of the Eagles

Though he goes nameless in The Hobbit, *it has long been suspected that the Lord of the Eagles and Gwaihir, the leader of the Great Eagles in* The Lord of the Rings, *are in fact the same bird. However, in* The Return of the King, *Gandalf says that he has been carried by Gwaihir twice before. If he were in fact the same Lord of the Eagles, the proper count would be three, including the rescue from the wargs in* The Hobbit. *Though it is difficult to say where the "other" Lord of the Eagles might have gone, one could argue that if Tolkien had intended them to be the same bird, he simply would have said so.*

72. When the eagles take Thorin's party to their eyrie, it is not the first time the Lord of the Eagles and Gandalf meet. What did Gandalf do for the Lord of the Eagles to become his friend?

○ **A.** Rescued him from orc captivity

○ **B.** Healed him from an arrow wound

○ **C.** Mended a broken wing

○ **D.** Helped him fend off an attack of Hell-hawks

73. In *The Lord of the Rings*, we learn that Elrond is a bearer of one of the three elven rings. Who are the other two bearers of elven Rings of Power?

_____

74. According to the elves, the dwarves have no life beyond the death of their bodies.

○ **A.** True.

○ **B.** False.

75. What is the name of the native tongue of the dwarves?

_____

76. Just as there are many kinds of elves in Middle-earth, there are many kinds of dwarves as well. What kind of dwarves are Thorin and company?

_____

77. Gandalf the Grey is the most powerful wizard in his Order.

○ **A.** True.

○ **B.** False.

78. Though he is known by many names to many different people, what is Gandalf's real name, given to him during his youth in Valinor?

_____

79. An outburst from Saruman in *The Two Towers* reveals the number of wizards in Middle-earth. Including Gandalf and Saruman, how many are there?

_____

80. More than 120 years before Bilbo was born, Thorin helped put an end to the War of Orcs in what battle before the East-gate of Moria?

_____

ÐWARVES, ELVES, AND HEROES

The dwarves of The Hobbit *come off poorly in a number of places in the book:*

- *In almost any dangerous situation, they're quick to push the hobbit forward to face it first*
- *Thorin is highly ungrateful to Mr. Baggins after his rescue from the dungeons of the Elvenking*
- *Only one—Balin—agrees to accompany Bilbo inside the secret passageway into the Lonely Mountain*
- *Thorin threatens to kill Bilbo after learning that the hobbit has given the Arkenstone to Bard*

With all of this, it's nice to see that Thorin asks Bilbo's pardon in the end and Balin comes to the Shire for a visit.

It's even nicer to know that Tolkien rethought and reworked elements of his characterization of the dwarves as a race when it came to writing The Lord of the Rings. *Gimli, representing the dwarves in the Fellowship, behaves with notable heroism, particularly at the Battle of Helm's Deep, where he kills forty-two orcs. He is shown to possess considerable lore, particularly concerning his own people. Most astonishingly, he becomes fast friends with Legolas Greenleaf, an elf, and loses his heart to Galadriel during the company's stay in Lothlórien. This friendship between an elf and a dwarf is so surprising that others remark on it (people of Minas Tirith stare in amazement at Gimli and Legolas when they walk through the city's streets). At the very end of the story, when Aragorn, King Elessar, has passed away, Legolas builds a ship and, together with his friend Gimli, sails into the Utter West, leaving Middle-earth forever.*

81. There are no female characters in *The Hobbit.*

○ **A.** True.

○ **B.** False.

ARAGORN DÚNADAN

Although Bilbo's adventure and Frodo's take place nearly eighty years apart, it is still possible that Bilbo could have met Aragorn the first time he visited Rivendell. Aragorn is an Númenórean, or what the elves call the Dúnedain, a race of men blessed with long life. After Aragorn's father, Arathorn, was slain, Aragorn was raised by Elrond in Rivendell and would have stood out in Bilbo's eyes as a young boy among elves.

82. Where is Arwen, Lord Elrond's daughter, when Bilbo and the dwarves pass through Rivendell?

_____

83. Following the Battle of Five Armies, the Lord of the Eagles becomes the King of All Birds.

○ **A.** True.

○ **B.** False.

84. Match the type of bird to the people with whom they share the closest relationship:

A. Ravens   **i.** Dwarves

B. Eagles   **ii.** Elves and men

C. Thrushes   **iii.** Men of Dale

85. Like Gimli in *The Lord of the Rings*, and Thorin himself, the dwarves of Thorin's party are all natural warriors.

  ○ **A.** True.

  ○ **B.** False.

86. Gandalf rides on a white horse in the early scenes of *The Hobbit*, but it is not the most well-known white horse he ever rides. What is that horse's name?

  _____

87. Thorin Oakenshield had no heir, and with his death and the death of his nephews, his line was ended.

  ○ **A.** True.

  ○ **B.** False.

88. How are the powers of a wizard of Middle-earth channeled?

  _____

89. Gandalf did not tell Thorin before the start of their quest that he had met Thráin because the time was not yet right; timing is of the essence for a wizard.

  ○ **A.** True.

  ○ **B.** False.

FAMILY HONOR

One curiosity of The Hobbit *is the appearance of Dain and Thorin's breth-ren from the Iron Hills, an apparently prosperous settlement only a relatively close 250 miles away from the Lonely Mountain. Why would Thorin and his people not join the other dwarves in the Iron Hills and instead live in sup-posed poverty far to the west? And why would Dain have not moved on the Lonely Mountain before the Battle of Five Armies? One answer is, of course, Smaug. Another is birthright: The Lonely Mountain and its treasures were Thorin's by rights, not Dain's. And the last, perhaps biggest, reason is fam-ily honor. Thorin would not have relinquished his kingdom in exchange for squatting in his cousin's halls without first fighting for his own.*

90. Though there is very little physical description of the dwarves, what feature of Fili's indicates that he and his brother, Kili, are not in fact identical twins?

_____

91. In accordance with his name, Gandalf the Grey's pointed hat and flowing cloak were both grey.

○ **A.** True.

○ **B.** False.

92. What is the name of Bard's grandson, who dies fighting alongside Dain Ironfoot in the Battle of Dale during the War of the Ring?

_____

93. What title does the Elvenking bestow upon Bilbo during his journey home through Mirkwood?

_____

94. Frodo and Bilbo share the same birthday (though seventy-eight years apart).

  ◯ **A.** True.

  ◯ **B.** False.

95. Perhaps because they stick to the road, Bilbo and his companions never meet this enigmatic ally from the valley of the Withywindle, as Frodo later does on his journey. What is his name?

_____

Chapter 2 Answer Key

1.	Old Took, Bilbo's grandfather on his mother's side.	23.	Thráin, Thorin's father.
2.	Grimbeorn.	24.	The White Council, presumably summoned by Saruman the White.
3.	Balin.	25.	Beorn.
4.	He was of the race of Dale.	26.	False. It is Thráin the Old who founds the dwarf kingdom under the Mountain in 1999 of the Third Age.
5.	C.		
6.	Fili and Kili.	27.	False. They are all derived from the poem.
7.	Radagast.	28.	"Völuspá" or "The Prophecy of Seeress."
8.	A.	29.	Elves and men.
9.	Light-elves, Deep-elves, Sea-elves.	30.	Bifur, Bofur, and Bombur.
10.	False. The Hobbit tells us that beeches are their favorite.	31.	Inconclusive! Though many suspect this is the case, there is no substantial evidence to confirm it, and Tolkien himself never says so explicitly.
11.	B.		
12.	False. Bilbo could not manage the wine barrels. The dwarves rode down the river in empty food barrels.	32.	Mead.
13.	Balin.	33.	False. Tolkien never states that elves have pointy ears in The Hobbit or in The Lord of the Rings.
14.	False. Their language was a secret one, spoken only between dwarves.	34.	Thranduil.
15.	True.	35.	Bladorthin.
16.	True.	36.	True.
17.	Carc.	37.	Seven.
18.	Dwalin.	38.	False. They greet them with music and song.
19.	False. Mithril mail is extremely rare and valuable.		
20.	The Wood-elves.	39.	True.
21.	Orcrist, which he took from Thorin while captive.	40.	False. Tharkûn is Gandalf's dwarvish name.
22.	False. Bard becomes the new King of Dale.	41.	Legolas.
		42.	The Istari (Wizards is also acceptable).

43.	Bear.	68.	Beornings.
44.	Balin and Dwalin.	69.	True. Shape-shifters do not hunt or eat any creature.
45.	Fili and Kili.	70.	True. The Elvenking defends his kingdom in Mirkwood and fends off an attack from Dol Guldur, Sauron's stronghold in Mirkwood.
46.	B.		
47.	D.		
48.	Gloin.	71.	Bard II.
49.	True.	72.	B.
50.	A.		
51.	Red wine.	73.	Mithrandir and Galadriel.
52.	Yellow.	74.	True.
53.	True.	75.	Khuzdul.
54.	D.	76.	Longbeards.
55.	False. They are known as "Durin's Folk."	77.	False. Saruman the White was the most powerful, though it is unclear how Gandalf the Grey matches up with the rest of the wizards.
56.	False. He merely loaned them the ponies and made it clear he wanted them returned, unharmed. He followed them to ensure the safety of his investment.	78.	Olórin.
57.	A.	79.	Five, although two are unaccounted for in Tolkien's works.
58.	A thrush.	80.	The Battle of Dimrill Dale (also known as The Battle of Azanulbizar, or The Battle of Nanduhirion).
59.	"Far Over the Misty Mountains Cold."		
60.	Dain.	81.	True, though women are mentioned in Lake-town, as are female hobbits in the Shire.
61.	B.		
62.	Bow and arrow.	82.	In Lórien, with Lady Galadriel.
63.	False. They got along well and thrived prior to Smaug's arrival.	83.	True, although it is unclear who was the King of All Birds before him.
64.	Bree.	84.	A-i, B-ii, C-iii.
65.	Dori.	85.	False. In fact, most of them were mere dwarf citizens under Thorin, or blacksmiths by trade.
66.	Red.		
67.	Aragorn.	86.	Shadowfax.

87.	True. However, Thorin III ruled in his stead, the son of his cousin, Dain Ironfoot.
88.	Through his staff.
89.	False. He hadn't told Thorin because he had not yet met him and did not know where he was.
90.	His long nose.

91.	False. His hat was blue.
92.	Brand.
93.	Elf-friend, or Bilbo the Magnificent.
94.	True.
95.	Tom Bombadil.

Score Your Ally Accreditation!

In this section, there are 97 possible right answers.

If you got 0–34 right, you're almost certainly a stone-giant: you make a lot of noise, and are about as friendly as you are bright.

If you got 35–65 right, you're a dwarf. Loyal and durable, but hardheaded and prone to getting yourself into tight spots.

If you got 66–97 right, you are a member of the White Council. Maybe you're not quite Gandalf, but being a wizard is still pretty awesome.

CHAPTER 3

VILLAINS AND ENEMIES

Middle-earth is a dark and dangerous place. Beyond the quaint, quiet safety of the Shire, Bilbo and his companions encounter all manner of foul creatures: some misunderstood, some inherently evil, and many that would prefer to eat halflings first and ask riddles later.

Though his journey provides plenty of reminders that the world beyond the Shire is no place for a hobbit, Bilbo proves surprisingly resilient against even the nastiest of enemies. He even manages to prove himself to his battle-tested companions. His courage overcomes his meager stature, and his cleverness proves more powerful than a sharp blade.

Then again: against trolls, goblins, orcs, giant wolves and spiders . . . it doesn't hurt to have a sharp blade.

But combat does still have its limits. The beast at the center of Bilbo's quest is Smaug, an ancient and cunning dragon who lives inside the Lonely Mountain atop a bed of treasure. He has terrorized dwarves, goblins, and men for many ages before coming face-to-face with his first hobbit. Against such powerful evil, what chance could an inexperienced halfling hope to have?

A scarier consideration is that the worst enemies of Middle-earth's civilized inhabitants are sometimes each other: dwarf against elf, and man against man, waging wars over riches, vanity, honor, and power. Perhaps monsters and evil obstacles are necessary in order to set aside such petty arguments and unite races in the name of good.

Or perhaps all it takes is a hobbit.

1. Gandalf reminds Thorin that the dwarf's grandfather, Thrór, after surviving Smaug's attack on the Lonely Mountain, was killed in the mines of Moria. Who killed Thrór?

_____

2. The Great Goblin, a Goblin King, had one distinguishing feature. What was it?

○ **A.** His red eyes

○ **B.** His huge head

○ **C.** His dwarf-forged crown

○ **D.** His stench

3. In _The Hobbit_, who (or what) did Gollum refer to as "my precious"?

_____

4. Which of these did Gollum _not_ keep in his pockets?

○ **A.** Fish bones

○ **B.** Goblins' teeth

○ **C.** The ring

○ **D.** A sharp stone to sharpen his fangs

5. Gollum claims to have received the ring on a very special day. When was it?

_____

6. What chilling shriek of Gollum's was only added to the text of _The Hobbit_ by Tolkien some ten years after he had originally drafted the chapter in which it appears?

_____

7. Chapter VI of _The Hobbit_ is called "Out of the Frying-Pan Into The Fire." Complete the following analogy: FRYING PAN : FIRE :: GOBLINS :

_____

8. As Bilbo and the dwarves are crossing the black stream in Mirkwood, something runs past them, knocking Bombur into the water. What is it?

_____

9. As Bilbo fights the giant spiders and struggles to free the dwarves, one thing he does especially angers the giant spiders. What is it?

_____

DRAGON STRAINS

In Middle-earth, there were once three different strains of dragon. The Urulóki were fire-drakes of the North. They could not fly, but could (as the name indicates) breathe fire. They were most common in the First Age. The second type, cold-drakes, lived only in the Ered Mithrin. It is unclear if they could fly, but they probably did not breathe fire. Smaug was the third kind of dragon: a winged dragon. They could fly, as well as breathe fire.

10. What are the only living things upon which Wood-elves have no mercy?

_____

11. What is the name of the Elvenking's butler, who has a bit too much to drink and allows Bilbo and the dwarves to escape?

_____

12. After attacking the party's camping site on the slopes of the Lonely Mountain, how many of the party's ponies did Smaug eat?

_____

13. What powerful magical artifacts is it rumored that dragon fire could consume?

_____

14. Bolg of the North, the leader of the goblin army during the Battle of Five Armies, is the brother of Azog, who took Moria.

  ○ **A.** True.

  ○ **B.** False.

15. If you cut them, do orcs not bleed? Sure they do—but what color is it?

_____

16. What large goblins (orcs) does Saruman breed as his personal fighting force in the War of the Ring?

_____

17. The sword Glamdring was also known as "the Foe-hammer." By what name did the goblins know it?

_____

The Scouring of the Shire

In The Return of the King, *Frodo and his hobbit companions return to find the Shire tainted by the spirit of Mordor and controlled by evil men. Merry and Pippin lead the hobbits in the Battle of Bywater, the last battle of the War of the Ring. Nineteen hobbits die, but the inhabitants of the Shire are victorious in driving out the evil. This event, however, has been left out of all film adaptations of* The Lord of the Rings, *perhaps because it is a dark thought to see the pristine Shire tainted, or exhausting to consider another hardship for the hobbits after all they have been through.*

18. The sword Orcrist was also known as "Goblin-cleaver." What did the goblins call it?

_____

19. Wargs, introduced in *The Hobbit*, make appearances later in *The Lord of the Rings* during the Battle of Helm's Deep. They are *not* known to do which of the following?

○ **A.** Outrun ponies

○ **B.** Raid settlements of men

○ **C.** Climb trees

○ **D.** Let orcs ride them

20. What are the colors of the banners carried by Bolg's army in the Battle of Five Armies?

_____

21. An early poem of Tolkien's described a creature very similar to Gollum. What was his name then?

○ **A.** Glop

○ **B.** Glip

○ **C.** Gollum

○ **D.** Bilbo

22. *Gull* or *goll* is Norse for "raw fish."

○ **A.** True.

○ **B.** False.

The STONE-TROLLS

Though they appear in the first of Peter Jackson's Hobbit *films, the three stone-trolls, Bert, William, and Tom, have been seen on the silver screen before: In* The Fellowship of the Ring, *after Frodo is stabbed by the Morgul blade of the Witch-king, Aragorn leads the hobbits to Rivendell. In the film version, they make a stop in the woods where Aragorn gives Frodo to Arwen in a race to save his life. It is there that they are standing in the shadows of "Mr. Bilbo's trolls," as Sam calls them. The extended version of the film gives a much better view of the trolls.*

23. During his riddle game with Bilbo, what does Gollum remember teaching his grandmother?

    ○ **A.** How to tell time

    ○ **B.** How to fish

    ○ **C.** How to suck eggs

    ○ **D.** How to cook

24. What kind of clothes is Gollum wearing when Bilbo meets him in the goblin caves?

_____

25. There is only one use of the word "orc" in the original text of *The Hobbit*. Tolkien didn't use the term fully until *The Lord of the Rings*.

    ○ **A.** True.

    ○ **B.** False.

26. Which of the following is *not* a name that Bilbo calls the giant spiders?

   ○ **A.** Insect

   ○ **B.** Attercop

   ○ **C.** Tomnoddy

   ○ **D.** Lob

27. In whose dungeons did Gandalf find Thorin's father, incoherent and without much of his memory?

_____

28. In *The Lord of the Rings*, the true name of the Necromancer is revealed. What is it?

_____

29. What, as revealed in *The Fellowship of the Ring*, was Gollum's real name?

_____

30. Whom did Gollum murder in order to take the ring?

_____

31. Before obtaining the ring, Gollum was actually of a race related to the hobbits.

   ○ **A.** True.

   ○ **B.** False.

32. Goblins are known for stealing ponies, donkeys, and horses for their own use. What do they usually do with them?

_____

33. Goblins hate the dwarves more than any other race.

○ **A.** True.

○ **B.** False.

GOBLIN EVOLUTION

It took some time for Tolkien to settle on the history of the origins of his goblins and orcs. He toyed with several different ideas related to their creation. These included the idea that they were lesser spirits corrupted by the evil spirit Morgoth (who also corrupted other angelic spirits to become the balrogs); and the idea that some of the goblins/orcs were created in this way, and they then procreated with other species. In The Silmarillion _he settled on the idea that the orcs are the corruption of elves who were carried off by Morgoth from the awakening place._

_In_ The Two Towers, _Treebeard, concerned by the appearance of orcs who can withstand the sunlight and appear bigger and stronger than their counterparts, speculates that Saruman either corrupted men to become orcs or he blended orcs and men into a hybrid race. Either seems possible, although the true solution will never be known, since the Uruk-hai are all destroyed during the downfall of Mordor._

Whatever the case, Sauron certainly has some means of continually producing orcs. According to Gandalf, most of the goblins of the Misty Mountains were scattered or destroyed during the Battle of Five Armies. Yet by the time of the events of The Lord of the Rings, _their numbers seem to have been substantially renewed. Further, Sauron has thousands of orcs to throw against the walls of Minas Tirith in the Battle of the Pelennor Fields._

So there must be an orc production line somewhere.

34. Fill in the blank: "[The goblins] make no beautiful things, but they make many _____ ones."

35. How many parts of the goblin warriors of the North perish during the Battle of Five Armies?

_____

36. Which dwarf was the first to receive a Ring of Power?

_____

37. In the very earliest versions of *The Hobbit* manuscript, what was the dragon's name?

_____

38. How many teeth does Gollum have?

_____

39. Though Smaug was the greatest dragon of the Third Age, what dragon in the Second Age was so large that its body crushed Thangorodrim, the highest peak in the Iron Mountains, when it was slain?

_____

40. What other animal sound are dragons said to make?

_____

41. Bilbo avoids giving Smaug his name because he doesn't want the dragon to attack the Shire.

○ **A.** True.

○ **B.** False.

42. What language do the orcs typically speak?

_____

43. It is said that if you look directly into its eyes, a dragon can control your mind.

○ **A.** True.

○ **B.** False.

44. Which of these is _not_ a nickname for Smaug?

○ **A.** Smaug the Golden

○ **B.** Smaug the Horrible

○ **C.** The Dragon Dread

○ **D.** Smaug the Magnificent

45. The year before *The Hobbit* was published, Tolkien read a paper before the British Academy concerning a famous literary monster. What was the name of the monster?

_____

46. Before he obtains his sword, Sting, Bilbo is captured by three trolls. Their names are Ted, Bart, and William.

○ **A.** True.

○ **B.** False.

47. When Bilbo is discovered by the three trolls, he identifies himself as:

○ **A.** A hobbit

○ **B.** An orc

○ **C.** A burrow hobbit

○ **D.** A burrahobbit

48. After "stinging" these creatures, Bilbo names his elvish short sword "Sting."

_____

49. In the first edition of *The Hobbit*, Tolkien commonly used the term "goblins," which he gradually replaced with "orcs" in later editions and other works.

○ **A.** True.

○ **B.** False.

AN ANCIENT QUARREL

The Elvenking holding the dwarves hostage—and treating them as enemies without charge of a crime—is not entirely unreasonable. In The Silmarillion *it is said that the dwarves and elves once went to war in ancient days over a dispute over payment: The elves accused the dwarves of stealing their treasure, while the dwarves accused the elves of hiring them to shape their raw gold and silver, then refusing pay once the work was complete. Eventually, the dwarves murdered the elf king, King Thingol of Doriath, over the dispute.*

50. Which of these actors has *not* provided the voice of Smaug in an adaptation of *The Hobbit*?

○ **A.** James Horan

○ **B.** Tony Jay

○ **C.** Richard Boone

○ **D.** Benedict Cumberbatch

51. According to Tolkien's phonology, the *au* sound is pronounced as *ow*, like *found* or *house*. Therefore, Smaug's name is not pronounced "*Smog*," but "*Sm-ow-g*."

○ **A.** True.

○ **B.** False.

52. If he wins the game of riddles, what does Gollum want from Bilbo?

_____

53. Before being captured by giant spiders, why do Bilbo and the dwarves leave the path and venture into the woods?

_____

54. The orcs use only weapons they've found or stolen from dwarves.

○ **A.** True.

○ **B.** False.

55. Though dragon underbellies are typically soft and vulnerable, Smaug's is protected by a dark enchantment.

○ **A.** True.

○ **B.** False.

56. When speaking to the dragon, Bilbo tells Smaug he and the dwarves have come for something other than treasure. What is it?

_____

57. Before beginning their journey, Bilbo tells Gandalf and the dwarves that he is willing to "walk from here to East of East and fight" what creatures?

_____

58. Smaug's bed is made completely of the treasure of the dwarves.

○ **A.** True.

○ **B.** False.

59. Like the trolls who capture Bilbo and the dwarves, all trolls in Middle-earth turn to stone in the sunlight.

○ **A.** True.

○ **B.** False.

60. What are the colors of Smaug's fire breath?

61. According to *The Quest of Erebor*, Gandalf wanted to see to it that Smaug was killed because he didn't want him to be used as a weapon of the Dark Lord in the coming wars.

○ **A.** True.

○ **B.** False.

62. In Middle-earth, a dragon is also known as a "Great Worm."

○ **A.** True.

○ **B.** False.

63. The great spiders in Mirkwood are thought to be the offspring of this spider, which Frodo and Sam encounter in *The Two Towers*.

SARUMAN'S TREACHERY

The renegade Saruman's turnabout from White Wizard to weapon of Sauron is a surprising and critical blow in the opening stages of the War of the Ring in The Lord of the Rings. *However, according to Gandalf's own telling of the events of* The Hobbit, *found in Tolkien's* Unfinished Tales, *the seeds of Saruman's treachery were planted well before the One Ring was identified. Gandalf recalls that Saruman disapproved of Gandalf's fondness for the halflings' "leaf" (pipe-weed) and hindered important business meetings even as early as the meeting of the White Council, for which Gandalf departs Thorin's party at the mouth of Mirkwood.*

64. All of the great spiders Bilbo encounters in Mirkwood are about as large as the one Frodo and Sam encounter in *The Two Towers*.

○ **A.** True.

○ **B.** False.

65. In ancient times, an evil spirit took the form of a spider and bred with the spiders of Middle-earth, producing the first of the great spiders. What is this evil spirit's name?

_____

66. The stone-giants of the Misty Mountains are not bothered by a mere thunderstorm. Instead of hiding in a cave, what do they do?

_____

67. Though they don't appear in *The Hobbit*, there are both were-wolves and vampires in Middle-earth.

O **A.** True.

O **B.** False.

68. When Gandalf heads south to Dol Guldur, after Bilbo and the dwarves enter Mirkwood, he already knows the identity of the Necromancer.

O **A.** True.

O **B.** False.

69. Of the race of trolls, only stone-trolls can speak in Westron, as the ones Bilbo encountered did.

O **A.** True.

O **B.** False.

70. They are known as Wood-elves in the Common tongue, but what is their proper Elvish name?

_____

71. Though more numerous, Wood-elves are not of the Eldar and are therefore less wise in spirit and body than the Three Kindreds.

O **A.** True.

O **B.** False.

72. What are the names of Bilbo's cousins who were primed to move into Bag End when he was presumed dead?

_____

73. In what year of the Second Age was the One Ring forged?

_____

74. The Master of Lake-town alienates his people for leaving the town in its time of need. Whom does he blame in order to deflect attention from himself for the town's destruction?

_____

75. Smaug is unique among dragons, having mastered the Common language (and therefore his ability to communicate with Bilbo).

○ **A.** True.

○ **B.** False.

76. "Smaug" is derived from the primitive Germanic verb *smugan*, meaning "to squeeze through a hole."

○ **A.** True.

○ **B.** False.

77. To which of the three strains of hobbits does Gandalf speculate that Gollum was probably related?

_____

melkor/morgoth

Though there are a great many villains and foul beasts in Middle-earth, nearly all of them can be traced back to one being. He is credited with creating orcs, balrogs, dragons, trolls, and wargs, among others. Even Sauron— the perceived central threat in the Lord of the Rings series—was once servant to him, and it is to his spirit that Sauron and the men he corrupts give their worship. His history of darkness is long and ancient, dating back to before the First Age and the creation of Middle-earth.

78. The effects of the enchantments of the black river in Mirkwood include drowsiness and night terrors.

○ **A.** True.

○ **B.** False.

79. Thráin was driven to leave his kingdom and reclaim the riches of the Lonely Mountain because he possessed a Ring of Power, which made him restless and discontented.

○ **A.** True.

○ **B.** False.

80. King Thingol of Doriath was an ancient elf king who was murdered by dwarves over what?

○ **A.** A dispute over payment for smithing services

○ **B.** The territory of the Grey Mountains

○ **C.** Stolen treasure

○ **D.** A betrayal in the Goblin Wars

81. In *Lord of the Rings*, Treebeard says that these creatures were created in "mockery" of Ents—though he also claims that Ents are much stronger. What are these creatures?

_____

82. Though several are killed by Gandalf, how many goblins do you calculate were present at the ambush in the cave, from Bilbo's description?

○ **A.** 14

○ **B.** 49

○ **C.** 86

○ **D.** 143

83. *Ent* means "troll" in Old English.

○ **A.** True.

○ **B.** False.

84. Tolkien briefly considered linking the origin of greater orcs to the balrogs and calling them "baldogs."

○ **A.** True.

○ **B.** False.

85. What is the name of the first dragon in Middle-earth, bred by Morgoth in the First Age (also known as the Deceiver)?

_____

BILBO'S TREACHERY

Many readers of The Hobbit *will recall that Bilbo turns the tide of the siege at the Lonely Mountain by taking Thorin's most prized treasure, the Arkenstone, to "the enemy" (Bard and the Elvenking) so they can use it as a bargaining chip. What is less often recalled, however, is that Bilbo took the great gem for himself and hid it from Thorin well before its value as a negotiating tool became obvious. Though Bilbo ultimately used the stolen gem for good, one wonders what he would have done with it had the opportunity never presented itself.*

86. Aside from being much greater in size, in what two ways are the great spiders of Mirkwood (and elsewhere in Middle-earth) different from everyday spiders?

_____

87. After killing Thrór, where did Azog carve Thrór's name as a mark of his accomplishment, igniting the War of the Dwarves and Orcs.

_____

88. The first fire-drake in Middle-earth was extremely powerful, but lacked one key attribute of later dragons. What was it missing?

_____

89. Which of these is a known ability of the orcs of the mountains?

    ○ **A.** Stooping incredibly low while running at great speeds

    ○ **B.** Catapulting themselves forward without a running start

    ○ **C.** Seeing clearly in the dark

    ○ **D.** Blacksmithing

90. What does Azog give to Thrór's companion in exchange for spreading the word to the other dwarves about Thrór's murder?

_____

91. After inheriting Moria from Azog, how long does Bolg rule the underground realm before he is finally slain in the Battle of Five Armies?

_____

92. Warg is an anglicized version of the Old Norse *vargr*. To what great and terrible Norse wolf does *vargr* usually refer?

_____

93. Though Tolkien only describes them as demonic wolves, what powerful scavengers do the wargs resemble in Peter Jackson's *The Lord of the Rings*?

_____

94. Dúnedain protect the Shire from orcs, trolls, and wargs, largely without the halflings' knowledge. What are these men called by the inhabitants of Bree and its environs?

_____

95. What weapon does Beorn give to the dwarves, one of which Thorin later uses to send away the messenger of the men at the Front Gate of the Lonely Mountain?

_____

how to make a dragon

Smaug was born from Tolkien's imagination, but he was also bred from several influential sources. The concept of a dragon purring, for example, came from a short story called "The Reluctant Dragon" by Kenneth Grahame (author of The Wind in the Willows_), of whom Tolkien was a fan. The dragon from_ Beowulf _and Fafnir of_ Vosunga _were both slain by attacks to their soft underbellies. And many of Smaug's boasts were derived from a passage concerning the Leviathan in the Book of Job._

Chapter 3 Answer Key

#	Answer	#	Answer
1.	Azog the goblin.	27.	The Necromancer.
2.	B.	28.	Sauron.
3.	Himself.	29.	Sméagol.
4.	C.	30.	Déagol, his cousin.
5.	On his birthday.	31.	True.
6.	"Thief, thief, thief! We hates it, we hates it, we hates it forever!"	32.	They eat them.
7.	Wargs.	33.	False. They didn't hate them any more than they hated everyone and everything else.
8.	A deer.		
9.	Calls them names.	34.	Clever.
10.	Giant spiders.	35.	Three.
11.	Galion.	36.	Durin III, the King of Khazad-dûm.
12.	Six.		
13.	Rings of Power.	37.	Pryftan.
14.	False. He is his son.	38.	Six.
15.	Black.	39.	Ancalagon the Black.
16.	Uruk-hai.	40.	Purr.
17.	Beater.	41.	False. The text says it is "unwise," though it is common in Germanic literature for dragons to be able to curse something using its name.
18.	Biter.		
19.	C.		
20.	Black and red.	42.	Orkish, mostly taken of other languages. When speaking to one another, different orc tribes spoke a debased form of Westron with bits of the Black Speech thrown in for good measure.
21.	B.		
22.	False. It is actually Norse for "gold," "treasure," "something precious," or "ring."		
23.	C.	43.	True.
24.	Tattered black clothing.	44.	B.
25.	True.	45.	Grendel, from the poem *Beowulf*.
26.	A.	46.	False. They are Tom, Bert, and William.
		47.	D.
		48.	Giant spiders.

49.	True.	72.	Otho and Lobelia Sackville-Baggins.
50.	B.	73.	1600.
51.	True.	74.	The dwarves.
52.	To let Gollum eat him.	75.	False. Dragons were skilled linguists in all ages of Middle-earth.
53.	To beg for food from the Wood-elves.	76.	True.
54.	False. They make their weaponry as well, but with much less craftsmanship than the elves or dwarves.	77.	Stoor.
55.	False. There is treasure stuck between his scales.	78.	False. It causes dreams that are actually quite pleasant, so much so that the afflicted prefer to stay sleeping.
56.	Revenge.	79.	True.
57.	Were-worms.	80.	A.
58.	False. Men and elves also had treasure taken by Smaug.	81.	Trolls.
59.	True.	82.	C.
60.	Green and red.	83.	False. It means "giant."
61.	True.	84.	True.
62.	True.	85.	Glaurung.
63.	Shelob.	86.	The great spiders have compound eyes, like insects; they also have stingers, while real-world spiders poison prey with their bite.
64.	False. They are smaller, though still quite large.	87.	Onto Thrór's brow.
65.	Ungoliant.	88.	Wings.
66.	Throw rocks and boulders at one another.	89.	A.
67.	True.	90.	A small pouch of money.
68.	True.	91.	About 150 years.
69.	True.	92.	Fenrir.
70.	Silvan elves.	93.	Hyenas.
71.	True.	94.	Rangers of the North.
		95.	Bow and arrow.

Score Your Enemy Education!

In this section, there are 95 possible right answers.

If you got 0–34 right, you must be from Mordor. We know Sauron runs a tight ship, but try to get outside of the Black Gates every now and then.

If you got 35–65 right, you belong in the Shire. Bright, clever, learned . . . but you prefer a bit of pipe-weed and a pint of ale to rigorous study.

If you got 66–95 right, you should make your way to Rivendell. Chat up the immortals, and browse the library. Perhaps retire and write a book: you're a rare mind.

CHAPTER 4

SETTINGS

𝔍n Tolkien's tales, the setting of Middle-earth is a character all its own. A whole cast of characters, in fact.

From the bucolic comforts of the hilly Shire, to the secluded majesty of Rivendell, or the foreboding shadow that is Mordor, geography reflects the lives of the inhabitants of Middle-earth, both physically and emotionally. Mountains, caves, rivers, and clearings provide characters with obstacles, shelters, landmarks, and tactical advantages.

To Tolkien, this was not an afterthought or a mere backdrop for his tale. The vistas of Middle-earth were carefully devised. He spent a considerable amount of time drawing maps of worlds to match the ones he imagined. The maps were so important, in fact, that he claimed "where this is possible and does not damage the story . . . take the maps as 'correct' and adjust the narrative."

One could even argue that *The Hobbit* is a classic tale of following a treasure map. The map Gandalf presents to Thorin, and which Thorin shows to Bilbo, motivates and guides the party's entire journey.

But where there are no maps, there is only memory. Can you find your way back to Middle-earth?

1. The map of the Lonely Mountain was made by Lord Elrond, of the elves.

   ○ **A.** True.

   ○ **B.** False.

2. What is the name of Elrond's home?

_____

3. Where were the great swords Glamdring and Orcrist, which the party retrieved from the trolls, originally made?

_____

4. The "heady vintage" of wine found in the Elvenking's cellar was made in and sent from Rivendell.

   ○ **A.** True.

   ○ **B.** False.

5. Fill in the blank: The area surrounding the Lonely Mountain was known as the "_____ of the Dragon."

6. What is the name of the river that flows from inside the Lonely Mountain, through the Dale, and down into the Long Lake?

_____

WINE AND ALE

The wine of Dorwinion on which the Wood-elves get drunk is said to be highly potent. Curiously, though, wine isn't a big feature of either The Hobbit *or* Lord of the Rings. *Hobbits generally prefer ale; Samwise Gamgee, in particular, makes frequent references to it, going so far as to take an extended swig from the beer barrel at Bag End before the start of the hobbits' journey. At the end of* The Return of the King, *when the Shire has been restored, one mark of its health is the excellence of its beer. Elves, in* The Lord of the Rings, *generally don't drink alcohol; they serve Frodo and his friends "a fragrant draught, cool as a clear fountain, golden as a summer afternoon."*

And then, of course, there is the drink of the Ents, which Pippin and Merry drink with astonishing results. But in general, there is no wine.

Perhaps it's just the more frivolous Wood-elves of Mirkwood who indulge in the heady wines of the south. In any case, Gandalf seems to have picked up their taste for wine—red wine, anyway—since he and Thorin ask for it when they arrive at Bilbo's hobbit-hole. The very fact that Bilbo can serve it to them means that wine wasn't unknown in the Shire; perhaps it was just saved for their guests instead.

7. The secret passage into the Lonely Mountain is five feet high and allows for how many people to walk abreast?

_____

8. The town on the shore of the lake near the Lonely Mountain was once known as "Dale."

○ **A.** True.

○ **B.** False.

9. What was the capital settlement of the goblins of the North?

_____

10. When is teatime in the Shire?

_____

11. What is the name of the mountain range that the party must cross, which lies between Rivendell and the Wilderland?

_____

12. The goblins have a special name for the "cave" in the mountains where the party takes refuge from the storm. What is their name for the cave?

_____

13. The Grey Mountains lie 200 miles north of Mirkwood. According to Gandalf, what danger lies to the south?

_____

14. Match the race to the attributes of its underground dwelling.

A. Hobbits   **i.** Deep, vast, geometric

B. Wood-elves   **ii.** Deep, dark, labyrinthine

C. Goblins   **iii.** Shallow, clean-smelling air

D. Dwarves   **iv.** Small, cozy, windowed

15. Lake-town was built on the lake to protect against Smaug's breath of fire.

  ○ **A.** True.

  ○ **B.** False.

16. By the end of *The Hobbit*, how many times has a Kingdom Under the Mountain been established?

  _____

17. What is the Elvish name for the Lonely Mountain?

  _____

18. What location shared its name with Tolkien's aunt's farm in Worcestershire?

  ○ **A.** The Shire

  ○ **B.** Bag End

  ○ **C.** Underhill

  ○ **D.** Hobbiton

19. According to Tolkien, Bag End means "cul-de-sac," or "the end of a path."

  ○ **A.** True.

  ○ **B.** False.

20. What is the name of the road that ends at Bilbo's hobbit-hole?

_____

21. In what great city was Bilbo's short sword, Sting, made?

_____

22. Though they are depicted as round doors with their knobs in the center in the live-action films, Tolkien actually describes a hobbit-hole door as having its knob to one side, like a proper door.

○ **A.** True.

○ **B.** False.

23. In what village is the Green Dragon, where Bilbo meets the dwarves prior to setting off on their adventure?

_____

24. Name the three original hobbit tribes of the Shire.

_____

25. What are the names of the two hobbits who founded the Shire?

_____

26. What township is the site from which the Mayor of the Shire presides over the Four Farthings?

_____

27. What dwarf kingdom did Balin go on to rule (albeit only for a short time) after the events of *The Hobbit*?

_____

28. What marks the path from Rivendell to Elrond's home?

_____

29. Bilbo and the dwarves cannot exit through the front door of the Wood-elves' cave because it is hidden and heavily guarded.

○ **A.** True.

○ **B.** False.

30. What special name is given to the western side of the southern spur of the Lonely Mountain?

_____

31. When the people of Lake-town rebuild their city, why do they not rebuild on the water?

- ○ **A.** There's no need after Smaug is dead
- ○ **B.** The spot where Smaug lands is considered cursed
- ○ **C.** It would be too trying
- ○ **D.** There aren't enough survivors

32. Prior to their migration and the establishment of the Shire, what were the ancestral lands of the hobbits?

_____

33. What is the name for the Shire in its inhabitants' dialect?

_____

34. In hobbit history, what name is given to the period between 1050 in the Third Age and the establishment of the Shire?

_____

35. In what year of the Third Age was the Shire established?

_____

36. What was the name of the king who gave the Hobbits permission to settle in the area of the Shire?

○ **A.** King Argeleb I

○ **B.** King Argeleb II

○ **C.** King Hador

○ **D.** King Tarondor

37. What was the dwarvish name of the mountain range where Thorin ruled?

_____

The Mines of Moria

The mines of Moria get an incidental mention at the beginning of The Hobbit *as the site of Thorin's father's death at the hands of Azog the goblin. They play a much more important role, of course, in* The Lord of the Rings.

Moria in its heyday was considered one of the wonders of the Northern World. Discovered by Durin, one of the dwarven Fathers, it became the vast underground city of Dwarrowdelf. As Gandalf explains in The Fellowship of the Ring, *it was also the only place in Middle-earth where mithril was found. The tragic attempt by Balin in the years following the events of* The Hobbit *to retake Moria and re-establish the dwarven kingdom there was doomed from the start. It occurred at a time when the orcs of the Misty Mountains were increasing as Sauron put forth his will from Mordor. It is unclear if Balin and his companions ever knew the true nature of the terror their forefathers had awakened in the deep, but in any case, it seems safe to say that if orcs hadn't gotten them in the short run, the balrog would have disposed of them in the long run.*

38. What is the Common name of the mountain range where Thorin ruled?

_____

39. What was the name of the hold where Gandalf found Thráin in the dungeons of the Necromancer?

_____

40. Into how many farthings is the Shire divided?

_____

41. What is the Elvish (Sindarin) name for the area Bilbo calls the "Wilderland"?

○ **A.** Rohan

○ **B.** Rhovanion

○ **C.** Rhudaur

○ **D.** Rimmon

42. In what direction do the Misty Mountains run?

○ **A.** North–South

○ **B.** East–West

○ **C.** Northeast–Southwest

○ **D.** Northwest–Southeast

43. What is the name of the river that flows parallel to the Misty Mountains, and passes beside the Carrock?

_____

44. Fill in the blank: The path that Bilbo and the party take from the Shire to the Edge of the Wild is known as "The Great _____ Road."

45. The name of the calendar used in *The Hobbit* is the Shire Calendar.

○ **A.** True.

○ **B.** False.

46. What is the name of the river, which goes unnamed in *The Hobbit*, over which Bilbo and the dwarves cross shortly before spotting the trolls' fire?

_____

47. What creatures did Bilbo and the dwarves notice on their walk up to Beorn's home, some "as big as thumbs"?

_____

48. Despite being built on the water, Lake-town was constructed entirely of wood and was therefore susceptible to dragon fire.

○ **A.** True.

○ **B.** False.

49. What race fought on Ravenhill during the Battle of Five Armies?

_____

50. "Mirkwood" is an ancient Germanic name that used to refer to the boundary between the Goths and the Huns.

○ **A.** True.

○ **B.** False.

51. According to Gandalf, what are shields used for in the Shire?

○ **A.** Cradles

○ **B.** Nothing

○ **C.** Saucers

○ **D.** Doors

52. Balin is the steward of Thorin's Hall.

○ **A.** True.

○ **B.** False

53. Gandalf tells Frodo that the _mithril_ mail Thorin gave Bilbo is worth more than all the Shire and everything in it.

○ **A.** True.

○ **B.** False.

54. What location was the dwarves' only source of _mithril_?

_____

55. Where was the One Ring forged?

_____

56. The name "Middle-earth" never appears in the *The Hobbit*.

   ○ **A.** True.

   ○ **B.** False.

57. What is the name of the planet where Tolkien's tales take place?

_____

58. Middle-earth is in fact one of two great continents in the realm. What is the name of the second?

_____

59. What is the proper name of the Western Sea, across which Bilbo and Frodo take their final voyage?

_____

60. Who named the Carrock, according to Gandalf?

_____

61. What is the name of the land between the Misty Mountains and the Blue Mountains, which includes the Shire?

_____

62. The river on which the Carrock is situated is the same river that the Fellowship of the Ring travels down by boat after leaving Lórien.

○ **A.** True.

○ **B.** False.

63. Mordor was the original domain of Sauron, although he attempted to establish other holds beyond the Black Gates in Middle-earth.

○ **A.** True.

○ **B.** False.

64. Before a shadow fell over Mirkwood, and again after the return of the king and the start of the Fourth Age, the great forest went by another name. What was it?

_____

65. Tunnels in hills suitable for hobbit-holes were known as "smials" in the Shire.

○ **A.** True.

○ **B.** False.

66. The Shire had a traditional ruler called the Thain, but its real leader was the Mayor. How frequently was an election for Mayor held?

_____

67. Though they have no uniforms and are only a dozen in number, the Shire has a police force known as the "Shirriffs."

○ **A.** True.

○ **B.** False.

68. Rivendell goes by another name in Elvish. What is it?

_____

69. Tolkien often used the names of real-world locations, such as China, before plugging in names for his imaginary locales.

○ **A.** True.

○ **B.** False.

70. The small, black boat that Bilbo and the dwarves use to cross the Black River in Mirkwood belongs to the Wood-elves.

○ **A.** True.

○ **B.** False.

71. Though its location is mentioned in the text, the elvish city of Dorwinion never appears on any of Tolkien's maps.

○ **A.** True.

○ **B.** False.

72. Time spent in an elvish forest or city always feels much longer than in reality.

   O **A.** True.

   O **B.** False.

73. What is the name of the land beyond the Grey Mountains, from which Smaug originally came?

_____

74. According to Lord Elrond, what evil forces destroyed the ancient elf city of Gondolin?

_____

75. What is the name of the dwelling of the Tooks, a network of tunnels at Tuckborough in the Shire?

_____

76. What was the name of the only person ever to live in Bag End who was _not_ a hobbit (though he occupied it without invitation or claim)?

_____

77. Though it is not quite where Bilbo and the dwarves encounter the trolls in _The Hobbit_, what is the name of the area near Rivendell where trolls are known to roam?

_____

78. With his attention focused on the realms of men and elves, Sauron did not know where the halflings dwelt when he first learned of their involvement with the One Ring.

   ○ **A.** True.

   ○ **B.** False.

79. What is the name of the river where Sméagol first obtains the One Ring?

_____

80. "Esgaroth" is Elvish for lily pads, which grew in abundance on the banks of the Long Lake.

   ○ **A.** True.

   ○ **B.** False.

81. This town is noted not only as an important crossroads, but also for being the only place where men and hobbits dwell together. What is its name?

_____

82. What was the name of the ancient kingdom that now lies in ruins between the river beneath the Last Bridge (from which Bilbo sees the trolls' fire) and Rivendell?

_____

83. In addition to supervising the Shirriffs, what other important service did the Mayor of the Shire oversee?

_____

84. Though the mines was poor in Thorin's time, the mountain range where his people dwelt was once home to two great dwarf cities in the First Age, which were destroyed in the Great Battle. Name them both.

_____

85. Where were Thráin and his company camped when he was captured and imprisoned in the Necromancer's tower?

_____

86. The Last Bridge over the Hoarwell that leads from the Great East Road to Rivendell (or to the Shire) goes by another, more formal, name. What is it?

_____

87. Prior to the Battle of Five Armies, Thorin calls on his cousin Dain to aid him. Where do Dain and his people come from?

_____

88. As a young widow, Tolkien's mother moved her family to this small hamlet just south of Birmingham, whose countryside became a major inspiration for the Shire.

_____

89. Fill in the blank: Dol Guldur, the hold of the Necromancer, is Sindarin for "Hill of _____."

90. After the War of the Ring, Galadriel tore down the walls of Dol Guldur, and it was taken over by her husband. What is his name?

_____

91. Other than Bywater, what is the closest town to Hobbiton, just around the hill?

_____

92. The mountain range where Thorin and his people live is actually divided in two by a great gulf. What is its name?

_____

93. The dwarves' party takes the same pass through the mountains as the Fellowship, only in the summertime and without Saruman as a hindrance.

  ○ **A.** True.

  ○ **B.** False.

94. The Long Lake is fed by two rivers. One is the Running River, which streams from the Lonely Mountain. What is the other?

_____

95. The Shire is only about 5,000 square miles, all told.

  ○ **A.** True.

  ○ **B.** False.

Chapter 4 Answer Key

1.	False. Lord Elrond helped interpret the map for Bilbo and the dwarves, but it was made by Thrór.	25.	Marcho and Blanco.
		26.	Michel Delving.
2.	The Last Homely House (or First Homely House, depending on the direction in which you're going).	27.	Khazad-Dûm.
		28.	White stones.
3.	Gondolin.	29.	False. It is sealed with magic.
4.	False. It was from Dorwinion.	30.	Ravenhill.
5.	Desolation.	31.	B.
6.	The Running River.	32.	The upper vales of the Anduin.
7.	Three.	33.	Sûza.
8.	False. It was known as Esgaroth.	34.	The Wandering Days.
9.	Gundabad.	35.	1601.
10.	4 P.M.	36.	B.
11.	The Misty Mountains.	37.	Ered Luin.
12.	The Front Porch.	38.	The Blue Mountains.
13.	The land of the Necromancer or Dol Guldur.	39.	Dol Guldur.
		40.	Four.
14.	A-iv, B-iii, C-ii, D-i.	41.	B.
15.	True.	42.	A.
16.	Three.	43.	The Anduin River.
17.	Erebor.	44.	East.
18.	B.	45.	True.
19.	True.	46.	Hoarwell.
20.	Hill Lane, where it ends (or just above Bagshot Road).	47.	Bees.
21.	Gondolin.	48.	True. Whoops.
22.	False. The doorknob is in the center.	49.	The elves.
23.	Bywater.	50.	True.
24.	Fallohides, Stoors, and Harfoots.		

51.	A.	75.	The Great Smials.
52.	False. Dwalin is the steward.	76.	Saruman.
53.	True.	77.	The Ettenmoors.
54.	Moria.	78.	True.
55.	Orodruin (Mount Doom).	79.	The Anduin near the Gladden Fields.
56.	True.	80.	False. It is Elvish for "reed lake," as reeds grow commonly on the banks of the Long Lake.
57.	Arda.
58.	Aman.	81.	Bree.
59.	Belegaer.	82.	Rhudaur.
60.	Beorn.	83.	The messenger service.
61.	Eriador.	84.	Belegost and Nogrod.
62.	True.	85.	The Wilderland, just under the eaves of Mirkwood.
63.	False. His original domain was Dol Guldur in southwestern Mirkwood.	86.	The Bridge of Mitheithel.
64.	Greenwood.	87.	The Iron Hills.
65.	True.	88.	Sarehole.
66.	Every seven years.	89.	Sorcery.
67.	True.	90.	Celeborn.
68.	Imladris.	91.	Underhill.
69.	True.	92.	The Gulf of Lhûn.
70.	False, or, at least, it is never made clear to whom the boat belongs.	93.	False.
71.	True.	94.	The Forest River.
72.	False. Though the time does seem to vary, it is always a matter of personal perception.	95.	False. It is about 18,000 square miles, or about half of the size of the state of Indiana.
73.	The Withered Heath.
74.	Dragons and goblins.

Score Your Settings Savvy!

In this section, there are 98 possible right answers.

If you got 0–34 right, you need to get out more. Don't be afraid to get lost!

If you got 35–65 right, you're an explorer. You've seen a bit of the world, but there's something holding you back . . .

If you got 66–98 right, you are an expert adventurer. You attack the world head-on, and relish the chance to see new places and meet new people—even if they try to kill you.

CHAPTER 5

The Hobbit in print

As epic as the story on the pages of *The Hobbit* is, the story of the pages themselves is nearly as remarkable.

Tolkien was merely a college professor with a knack for linguistics and an affinity for old tales, myths, and poems. He did not set out to become the father of modern fantasy. By the time *The Hobbit* was published (after years of slow development and intermittent writing), Tolkien was already well established in his career and had seen the birth of all four of his children. Even once the manuscript was complete, it took some prodding to get it out the door—much like Bilbo himself.

The Hobbit is also unique, given the scope of Tolkien's work. Though it was tremendously successful in its own right, nothing could prepare him for the world-renown that would come with the unprecedented notoriety of *The Lord of the Rings*. Sales of *The Hobbit* picked up, along with his other books and stories set in Middle-earth, and the rest is history. But this put his earlier work in a strange position: For one, *The Hobbit* and *Lord of the Rings* were not even in the same genre. Despite their connections in plot and setting, *The Hobbit* is very much a children's book in tone and execution. Moreover, much more thought, detail, and time went into *The Lord of the Rings*, and now *The Hobbit* is considered the world over as a "prequel."

Tolkien spent much of the rest of his life expanding the world of Middle-earth, and made many attempts to reconcile the two books from appendices to rewrites and beyond. How much do you recall about the history of *The Hobbit*?

1. In what year was *The Hobbit* first published?

   ○ **A.** 1927

   ○ **B.** 1937

   ○ **C.** 1947

   ○ **D.** 1957

2. *The Hobbit* borrows heavily from another Tolkien work that went unpublished until forty years after the earlier book's release. What is this work?

   _____

3. Tolkien claims that his vision of Gollum was vague only until he began to see illustrations of the character in foreign publications of *The Hobbit*.

   ○ **A.** True.

   ○ **B.** False.

4. What famous author was the first person to read Tolkien's original manuscript of *The Hobbit*?

   ○ **A.** Lewis Carroll

   ○ **B.** C.S. Lewis

   ○ **C.** John Steinbeck

   ○ **D.** Harper Lee

BILBO'S LIE

In the original printing of The Hobbit, *Gollum offers the ring to Bilbo as a reward for winning the riddle game. For later editions, however, Tolkien had to change this telling to make the tale accord with the greater lore of* The Lord of the Rings. *But Tolkien also made this major revision a part of the story: as* The Hobbit *is itself an adaptation of Bilbo's own book, it is later established that the influence of the ring led to Bilbo's "lie." Subsequent editions of Bilbo's tale, then, tell the "true" version of his encounter with Gollum.*

5. Who was the original publisher of *The Hobbit*?

_____

6. Which of these famous stories is *not* considered an inspiration for *The Hobbit*?

○ **A.** *The Princess and the Goblin*

○ **B.** *The Princess and Curdie*

○ **C.** *Beowulf*

○ **D.** *Rumpelstiltskin*

7. Though in traditional literature "hobgoblins" are a smaller form of a goblin, Tolkien describes them as the opposite: a larger-than-normal goblin.

○ **A.** True.

○ **B.** False.

PERMISSION TO RIDDLE

A decade after publication, publisher Allen & Unwin told Houghton Mifflin they could reproduce the riddles in Bilbo's and Gollum's exchange in a poetry anthology without Tolkien's permission because, according to them, "the riddles were taken from common folk lore and were not invented by you." Tolkien responded politely, but left no doubt that although several of the poems were derivations of "old literary (but not folk-lore) riddles," Houghton Mifflin could not lift his work without a fee.

8. There exists an account of the events of *The Hobbit* in which the story is told largely from Gandalf's perspective. What is it called?

_____

9. *The Hobbit* is considered the first Young Adult novel.

    O **A.** True.

    O **B.** False.

10. Which of the following is a curse word that appears in *The Hobbit* and was invented by Tolkien?

    O **A.** Attercop

    O **B.** Confusticate

    O **C.** Fandifferous

    O **D.** Farkle

11. During what year of the Third Age does the beginning of *The Hobbit* take place?

_____

12. Tolkien made significant changes to *The Hobbit* so that it would better fit with elements of *The Lord of the Rings*. What year were these changes first printed?

    ○ **A.** In 1939, the Second Edition of the book

    ○ **B.** In 1951, three years before *The Lord of the Rings*

    ○ **C.** In 1966, some dozen years after *The Lord of the Rings*

    ○ **D.** The changes were never printed

13. What is the name of the fictional book of tales that Tolkien claims is the source of his stories?

_____

14. A reference to the Lilliputians, a race much smaller than the hobbits, was dropped from later editions of the text.

    ○ **A.** True.

    ○ **B.** False.

15. Bilbo and Gollum ask each other the same number of riddles in Chapter V: Riddles in the Dark.

    ○ **A.** True.

    ○ **B.** False.

16. Tolkien was a linguist and a master of wordplay. Match the term to its definition.

A. Hobnob   i. To drink and gossip

B. Hobbyhorse   ii. Medieval dancer

C. Hobble   iii. To perplex

D. Hobbiler   iv. A farmer and a soldier

17. Tolkien originally described the hobbits' affinity for smoking "tobacco," but he later changed the name of the substance they smoked. What did he end up calling this substance?

_____

18. Along with his map, Thráin gives Gandalf the key to the back door of the Lonely Mountain. What material is the key made of?

_____

19. In order to reveal the secret runes on Thráin's map, Elrond holds it up to the light of the setting sun.

○ A. True.

○ B. False.

20. Wearing the One Ring, Bilbo is not completely invisible: He still casts a shadow.

○ A. True.

○ B. False.

The MOON-RUNES

Prior to publication of The Hobbit, Tolkien wondered about the best way to display Thrór's map and its hidden moon-runes, which were revealed by Elrond. He first thought of a watermark, which could be seen when held up to the light, but this would have been cost-prohibitive. Tolkien's next idea was to print the hidden runes in reverse on the backside of the map page. Unfortunately, publisher Allen & Unwin used both maps (with and without the runes revealed) on either inside cover of the first edition, but the "reverse runes" idea was finally executed in the 1979 edition.

21. Because they stuck to the road and were not chased by Ringwraiths, Bilbo and company traveled from Bag End to Rivendell much faster than Frodo did with the One Ring years later.

○ **A.** True.

○ **B.** False.

22. The "raft-men" who guided the barrels down the river to Lake-town were in fact elves, not men.

○ **A.** True.

○ **B.** False.

23. Which character from *The Lord of the Rings* was the only one to whom Tolkien later gave his own book?

_____

24. What American university is home to the original manuscript of *The Hobbit*?

_____

25. The scene of Bilbo stealing the great two-handed cup from Smaug pays homage to another famous story. What is it?

_____

26. Durin's Day occurs once a year.

○ **A.** True.

○ **B.** False.

27. Though themes abound in Tolkien's work, what is the recurring cardinal sin in his ethos?

_____

28. After the War of the Ring, Gandalf shares his account of the events of _The Hobbit_. Who writes them down?

_____

29. There are no references to female elves in _The Hobbit_.

○ **A.** True.

○ **B.** False.

30. The graphic novel of _The Hobbit_ is difficult to find because it was not approved by the Tolkien Estate and was pulled from shelves.

○ **A.** True.

○ **B.** False.

A Cheater and a Thief

There is, of course, much debate surrounding Bilbo's famed final "riddle," which, as it turns out, is not a riddle at all. Since much ado is made about the sanctity of the riddle game, it is surprising that Bilbo "wins" with such a simple deceit. However, a careful examination of the text reveals something more: when Gollum prods Bilbo for his final riddle, he says, "It's got to ask us a question." So you see, Bilbo might argue that Gollum simply got what he asked for.

31. Who drew *The Hobbit: An Illustrated Version of the Fantasy Classic*, a graphic novel?

_____

32. What company first published the comics comprising *The Hobbit: An Illustrated Version of the Fantasy Classic*?

○ **A.** Image Comics

○ **B.** DC Comics

○ **C.** Eclipse Comics

○ **D.** Ballantine Books

33. In what year was the first authorized adaptation of *The Hobbit* made?

○ **A.** 1938

○ **B.** 1953

○ **C.** 1989

○ **D.** 2012

34. What section of the book has become so well known that it made *Bartlett's Familiar Quotations* in 1971?

---

35. In Tolkien's original manuscript, the Lonely Mountain and Mirkwood were named the Dark Mountain and Blackwood, respectively.

○ **A.** True.

○ **B.** False.

36. Though Tolkien intended for the dwarves to have their own runic alphabet, he had not yet developed it when he wrote *The Hobbit*. The runes found on the map in *The Hobbit* are in fact Anglo-Saxon runes.

○ **A.** True.

○ **B.** False.

37. Elrond is never described as an elf in *The Hobbit*.

○ **A.** True.

○ **B.** False.

38. A discrepancy over whether Durin's Day was marked by the first or the last moon of autumn remained in Chapter IV of the text until 1995.

○ **A.** True.

○ **B.** False.

39. Approximately how many copies of the original first edition hardcover of *The Hobbit* were printed?

_____

40. Four hundred twenty-three copies of the original first edition hardcover print of *The Hobbit* were destroyed before they ever shipped. What was the reason for their destruction?

○ **A.** A bombing during the Battle of Britain

○ **B.** A warehouse fire

○ **C.** A printing error in which there were two copies of page 93 and no page 94

○ **D.** Water damage from a leaking roof

41. In a 1961 Puffin edition of *The Hobbit*, the printers famously made what "correction"?

○ **A.** They removed all of the slayings of goblins and the deaths during the Battle of Five Armies

○ **B.** They changed instances of "dwarves" to "dwarfs" (though they left "elves" the same)

○ **C.** They gave Bilbo a wife and three children to make the book more family-oriented

○ **D.** They have Bilbo slay Smaug

42. Other than Beorn, who comes alone, what "army" is not accounted for in the five armies of the Battle of Five Armies?

_____

The CURSE OF The DWARF kINGS

In Tolkien's famed illustration of the Kingdom Under the Mountain, which features Smaug upon his bed of treasures and Bilbo in silhouette, there is a large barrel in the foreground marked with the same runes as the dwarves' map. Though many of the runes are obscured or unseen, what is legible appears to offer a warning, roughly translating to: "Gold of Thrór and Thráin; accursed be the thief."

43. All but one of the elves who appear in *The Hobbit* go unnamed. What is this elf's name?

_____

44. Thrór's map that accompanies *The Hobbit* is only meant to be a copy of the map, drawn by Bilbo himself.

   ○ **A.** True.

   ○ **B.** False.

45. After publishing *The Hobbit*, Tolkien returned to his other works and did not begin work on *The Lord of the Rings* for another five years.

   ○ **A.** True.

   ○ **B.** False.

46. There are many poems or songs in *The Hobbit*, some of which have been used in adaptations of the story or set to music. How many poems in total can be found in *The Hobbit*?

○ **A.** 20

○ **B.** 23

○ **C.** 26

○ **D.** 29

47. With all of his errands and seemingly important business, why did Gandalf first accompany Thorin and company, according to his own recounting of the tale?

○ **A.** Thorin would only accept Bilbo's presence if Gandalf came to "look after" his "darling"

○ **B.** It was on his way

○ **C.** The dwarves were unskilled in battle and he knew they would need protection

○ **D** As he put it, "I was not particularly busy that year"

48. Gollum's unmistakable speech patterns and pronoun use disappear when he recites his riddles for Bilbo.

○ **A.** True.

○ **B.** False.

49. This popular children's book series of the 1920s was a favorite of the Tolkien children and greatly influenced Tolkien to include talking animals in *The Hobbit*.

50. *The Hobbit* was Tolkien's third published work for children, after *Mr. Bliss* and *Farmer Giles of Ham*.

   ○ **A.** True.

   ○ **B.** False.

51. This illustrated children's story about a man who wore tall hats and lived in a tall house was not published in the wake of *The Hobbit*'s success because the cost of color printing was prohibitive.

_____

52. In an early draft, Tolkien included a wayward knight to guard the bridge over the River Hoarwell.

   ○ **A.** True.

   ○ **B.** False.

53. Of all places, Tolkien's youngest son, Christopher, was educated at Dragon School, a prep school in Oxford.

   ○ **A.** True.

   ○ **B.** False.

54. *The Father Christmas Letters*, which Tolkien wrote for his children each Christmas, were edited by Baillie Tolkien, one of his son's wives, and published posthumously. To which of Tolkien's sons was Baillie married?

_____

SECOND EDITION

The second edition of The Hobbit *was not released until 1951, in preparation for the upcoming* The Lord of the Rings. *Tolkien wrote this version of* The Hobbit *as the foundation for* The Lord of the Rings, *and took pains to reconcile his "prequel" with his larger, more epic tale (especially with regards to Bilbo's exchange with Gollum). However, though he sent the suggested corrections to Allen & Unwin in 1947, Tolkien didn't actually think a new edition of his book was going to be released. Then, three years later, he received the page proofs from the publisher.*

55. What honorary appointment did Tolkien receive from Queen Elizabeth II on March 28, 1972?

_____

56. Tolkien once applauded (figuratively) a Swedish critic who read *The Lord of the Rings* as an anti-communist parable, with Stalin as Sauron.

○ **A.** True.

○ **B.** False.

57. How many volumes of the expansive *The History of Middle-earth* are there?

_____

58. The first print run of 15,000 copies of *The Hobbit* sold out by December—after release that same month.

○ **A.** True.

○ **B.** False.

59. A fact that would surely tickle Tolkien the linguist: *The Hobbit* has been translated into more than forty languages.

○ **A.** True.

○ **B.** False.

60. This two-volume work by John Rateliff breaks down and examines the text of *The Hobbit* at each stage of its existence—including the first hand-written manuscript pages and Tolkien's own personal plot notes. What is the name of the book?

_____

61. The publishers enjoyed Tolkien's original illustrations so much that they included them in the book without raising its price—and so Tolkien gave them five more. How many illustrations appear in the first edition of the book?

_____

62. The Children's Book Club edition of *The Hobbit*, printed in 1942, is the only version of the book printed with the illustrations but without the all-important maps.

○ **A.** True.

○ **B.** False.

63. Though there were no numbers on the front covers of the 1989 comic book adaptations, they were numbered on the spine. How many issues were there?

_____

64. In 2006, *The Hobbit* comics were published in a single edition with a new cover featuring lifelike interpretations of the characters. Who was the cover's artist?

_____

65. *The Hobbit* comics were drawn with one page for every page in the second edition of the book, totaling 317 pages.

○ **A.** True.

○ **B.** False.

66. *The Hobbit* comic book artist David Wenzel held a Tolkien art exhibition at Joseloff Gallery his junior year of college.

○ **A.** True.

○ **B.** False.

IN A PICKLE

During the opening chapter of The Hobbit, *as Bilbo juggles food orders from the dwarves, Gandalf implores him to "bring out the cold chicken and tomatoes!" Nearly thirty years after the original publication, Tolkien changed "tomatoes" to "pickles." Why? He recognized that tomatoes were foreign to England, the Shire of his mind, and therefore had no place in the Shire of Middle-earth. He similarly eradicated the word "tobacco," another foreign import, and in* The Lord of the Rings *tends to stick to "taters" rather than "potatoes."*

67. What UK magazine published a fifteen-part visual serial of *The Hobbit* from 1964 to 1965?

_____

68. The first editor of *The Hobbit* was Tolkien's wife, Edith, from whom he received notes whenever he finished a new section of the book.

○ **A.** True.

○ **B.** False.

69. Tolkien's famous original cover featuring the Lonely Mountain and Mirkwood originally included the colors of the setting sun, but the publisher had to reduce the illustration to three colors for printing. What three colors make up the cover?

_____

70. Before deciding to publish it, publisher Stanley Unwin gave the book to his ten-year-old son to review.

○ **A.** True.

○ **B.** False.

71. What publisher printed the unauthorized edition of *The Lord of the Rings* in 1960, prompting Tolkien to produce a new edition of *The Hobbit* in order to renew the copyright?

_____

72. *The Hobbit* makes use of interpolative narration, where the narrator frequently stops to address the reader. Tolkien dropped this style in *The Lord of the Rings*, but said late in life that he wished he had included more of it to better match the styles.

○ **A.** True.

○ **B.** False.

The missing edition

In 1960, with the popularity of The Lord of the Rings *in full swing, Tolkien returned to* The Hobbit *to bring the tone and language more in line with the style of his epic. After three chapters, an anonymous (though presumably someone close to Tolkien) critic told him that it was great, but it "just wasn't* The Hobbit." *He abandoned the changes and let sleeping dragons lie.*

73. When Tolkien returned to *The Hobbit* after completing *The Lord of the Rings*, he found it "very poor."

○ **A.** True.

○ **B.** False.

74. Though paperback copies of books now tend to follow within a few years of their hardcover editions, the first paperback of *The Hobbit* was not published by Puffin Books until what year?

_____

75. The illustrator of the cover of the first American paperback of *The Hobbit* drew her cover before reading the book. The cover includes lions and emus in the foreground.

○ **A.** True.

○ **B.** False.

76. In 2008, one of the original, first edition, first printing versions of *The Hobbit* was auctioned off at Bonhams in London. How much did it sell for?

○ **A.** £10,000

○ **B.** £30,000

○ **C.** £60,000

○ **D.** £140,000

77. The auctioned book referred to in Question 76 was inscribed to a friend of Tolkien's, who helped get it into the hands of Stanley Unwin, and subsequently published. Who was the friend?

_____

78. By some estimates, *The Hobbit* has sold more than 250 million copies to date worldwide.

○ **A.** True.

○ **B.** False.

79. Since Nielsen began keeping track of book sales in 1995, *The Hobbit* has not fallen below 5,000 in the top book rankings.

○ **A.** True.

○ **B.** False.

80. How old was Tolkien when *The Hobbit* was published?

_____

81. U.S. publisher Houghton Mifflin pulled an icon of Bilbo from one of Tolkien's illustrations for use on the cover and title page of its first edition. What was Bilbo wearing that forced them to stop using it in future editions?

_____

82. The icon referred to in Question 81 depicted a character playing a musical instrument. What is the instrument?

_____

83. Which of his sons did Tolkien employ to re-type changes and corrections into the working manuscript of *The Hobbit*?

_____

84. *The Hobbit* has been translated into dozens of languages over the years. In what language was *The Hobbit* first translated?

_____

85. In 1977, the filmmakers of the animated film produced a fully illustrated version of the book in the style of the movie. But the cover depicts an oddity: Smaug is flying somewhere he's never been. Where is it?

_____

PAPERBACK WRITER

When the first paperback edition of The Hobbit *was finally published, Puffin Books (an imprint of Penguin) printed a healthy run of about 35,000. However, they found out afterward that these copies could not be imported into the United States, possibly because of Houghton Mifflin's license in the States. Additionally, Allen & Unwin were concerned that their own hardcover sales would be hurt by the paperback and therefore would not allow a second printing, even after the books had sold out.*

86. When Tolkien published *The Hobbit*, his friend C.S. Lewis was motivated to write *The Lion, the Witch & the Wardrobe*.

○ **A.** True.

○ **B.** False.

87. To celebrate the seventy-fifth anniversary of *The Hobbit*'s publication, HarperCollins issued *The Art of the Hobbit*, collecting in a single volume for the first time all of the sketches, drawings, and paintings made by Tolkien for his book. How many of Tolkien's pieces were included in this volume?

○ **A.** 210

○ **B.** 190

○ **C.** 110

○ **D.** 300

88. What wildly popular 1960s children's book author and illustrator was invited by a publisher to try his hand at illustrating *The Hobbit* (although his drawings were firmly rejected by Tolkien)?

_____

89. Whom did Tolkien indicate in a 1959 letter that he was "not especially interested in writing for"?

_____

Chapter 5 Answer Key

1.	B.		24.	Marquette University.
2.	*The Silmarillion.*		25.	Beowulf.
3.	False. He actually took issue with the illustrations of Gollum, which tended to depict Gollum as some kind of hideous monster.		26.	False. The dwarves' year is the first day of the last moon cycle to begin in autumn. When the sun and the moon can be seen in the sky together on this day, it is Durin's Day.
4.	B.		27.	Pride.
5.	Allen & Unwin.		28.	Frodo.
6.	D.		29.	False. There is one reference.
7.	True.		30.	False.
8.	The Quest of Erebor.		31.	David Wenzel.
9.	False. It was published as a children's book, intended for children aged 6–10.		32.	C.
10.	B.		33.	B.
11.	2941 of the Third Age.		34.	The opening paragraph.
12.	B.		35.	False. They were named Black Mountain and Wild Wood.
13.	The Red Book of Westmarch.		36.	True.
14.	True.		37.	True. In fact, Bilbo makes separate mention of the elves, as if to suggest they were different or separate from their host.
15.	True, five each.		38.	True.
16.	A-i, B-iii, C-ii, D-iv.		39.	17,000.
17.	Pipe-weed.		40.	A.
18.	Silver.		41.	B.
19.	False. He holds it up to the moonlight.		42.	The eagles.
20.	True.		43.	Galion, the Elvenking's butler. Lord Elrond is only half elven.
21.	False. An examination of Tolkien's descriptions of the passage of time on their respective journeys indicates that Bilbo was traveling much slower than Frodo and Strider.		44.	True.
22.	True.		45.	False. He began work three months after *The Hobbit* was published; almost immediately.
23.	Tom Bombadil.			

46.	B.
47.	A.
48.	True, though this could be chalked up to the game being part of Bilbo's recollection and telling.
49.	*Dr. Dolittle.*
50.	False. These books were published after *The Hobbit*, in response to its success.
51.	*Mr. Bliss.*
52.	False. The obstacle was that there was no bridge and no way to get across.
53.	True.
54.	Christopher Tolkien.
55.	Commander of the Order of the British Empire.
56.	False. The reading was made, but Tolkien was fiercely anti-allegorical.
57.	Twelve.
58.	False. The first print run was only 1,500 copies. But it didn't sell out by December.
59.	True.
60.	*The History of The Hobbit.*
61.	Ten.
62.	True.
63.	Three.
64.	Donata Giancola.
65.	False. The comics are 133 pages long in total.
66.	True.
67.	*Princess and Girl.*
68.	False. The true first editors were Tolkien's children who, before bedtime, were its only audience for years.
69.	Green, blue, and black.
70.	True.

71.	Ace Books.
72.	False. He regretted the interpolative narration.
73.	True.
74.	1961.
75.	True.
76.	C.
77.	Elaine Griffiths.
78.	False. Though it has been estimated to have sold over 100 million copies worldwide.
79.	True.
80.	Forty-five years old.
81.	Boots.
82.	A flute.
83.	Michael.
84.	Swedish . . . presuming you don't count "American."
85.	The Misty Mountains.
86.	False. C.S. Lewis published his first novel, *The Pilgrim's Regress* in 1933.
87.	C.
88.	Maurice Sendak. The rejected image of Bilbo and Gandalf is held today by Yale University's Beinecke Rare Book and Manuscript Library.
89.	Children.

Score Your Publishing Perceptivity!

In this section, there are 92 possible right answers.

If you got 0–34 right, we strongly recommend you get yourself a library card. You know, libraries?

If you got 35–65 right, you're a regular book worm. Try not to get trapped out in the sun for too long.

If you got 66–92 right, you're a scholar. If they bottled the scent of old books, you would probably shower in the stuff.

CHAPTER 6

FILMS, VIDEO GAMES, AND OTHER ADAPTATIONS

A daptations of popular books are nearly as inevitable as they are impossible. On one hand, a book's popularity encourages creators to make film and video game versions of the work, and motivates the fan base to want them. On the other hand, the more beloved the story, and the more it relies on human imagination, the greater the odds that any adaptation will fall short of reader expectations.

In this regard, *The Hobbit* and *The Lord of the Rings* have seen more success than most. Tolkien and his estate have kept a careful watch over any and all products inspired by his books—you aren't likely to see a Gollum stuffed animal or a hobbit Saturday morning cartoon show any time soon. Though popular since their respective release dates, Tolkien's books soared into the cultural stratosphere in 2001 with the release of the first of five Peter Jackson films set in Middle-earth.

Before then, however, *The Hobbit* was the subject of many varied adaptations in its seventy-plus-year history. These included musicals, animated films, stage plays, board games, radio series, and even an opera. Though the core tale always remains the same, these adaptations have varying degrees of faithfulness and regard—but if you're a true fan, you'll know them. After all: who could resist the chance to accompany Bilbo on his adventure one more time?

1. What popular cartoon show parodied *The Hobbit* animated film in its episode "The Death Camp of Tolerance"?

_____

2. In the animated film, Thorin makes a toast to Bilbo. What is it?

○ **A.** "May all his burglaries reap gold."

○ **B.** "May he live to see his one hundred and eleventh birthday."

○ **C.** "May every man, dwarf, and hobbit across the land hear of his name."

○ **D.** "May the hair on his toes never fall out."

3. In his lifetime, this man received Oscar nominations for directing, writing, and acting. He was also the voice of Gandalf in the animated version of *The Hobbit*. Who is he?

_____

4. This American folk singer sang the main theme of the animated film with his trademark vibrato.

○ **A.** Bob Dylan

○ **B.** Glenn Yarbrough

○ **C.** Kenny Edwards

○ **D.** Johnny Cash

PETER JACKSON VERSUS NEW LINE CINEMA

In 2005, Peter Jackson filed a lawsuit against New Line Cinema, the studio behind The Lord of the Rings *films. The lawsuit intended to audit New Line regarding profits for merchandising and video games related to* The Fellowship of the Ring. *New Line co-founder Robert Shaye responded publicly that Jackson would never work with them again as long as he was at the company (which would mean Jackson's exclusion from* The Hobbit*). Shaye eventually ate his words, realizing Jackson's importance to the franchise. New Line Cinema settled the lawsuit and was fined $125,000 for failing to provide the requested accounting documents.*

5. What do the goblins in the animated film have that those in the book do not?

_____

6. In the animated film, how many dwarves survive the Battle of Five Armies?

_____

7. In what country was *The Hobbit* animated?

_____

8. The co-directors of the animated film also directed famed stop-motion holiday movies, such as *Frosty's Winter Wonderland, Santa Claus Is Comin' to Town,* and *Jack Frost.*

○ **A.** True.

○ **B.** False.

9. In *The Hobbit*, the significance of Bilbo's ring is not yet known, but in the animated film, Gandalf alludes to its importance and the adventures that are to come because of it.

○ **A.** True.

○ **B.** False.

10. The director of the live-action *The Lord of the Rings* trilogy, Peter Jackson, returned to direct *The Hobbit*, but he was originally only the producer. What director did he replace?

_____

11. What is the subtitle of the first live-action *Hobbit* film?

_____

12. This actor, who also played Magneto in the *X-Men* films, returned to the franchise to play Gandalf in *The Hobbit* films.

_____

13. All of the riddles asked by Bilbo and Gollum in the animated film are taken directly from the book.

○ **A.** True.

○ **B.** False.

14. The animated film's main musical theme, "The Greatest Adventure," was written by Tolkien but did not appear in *The Hobbit*.

○ **A.** True.

○ **B.** False.

15. What character appears in the book but not in the animated film?

_____

16. This elf, played by Evangeline Lilly, does not appear elsewhere in the *Lord of the Rings* universe and was invented solely for the live-action film.

_____

17. Which of the following make appearances in the live-action films, despite not appearing in *The Hobbit* (choose all that apply)?

○ **A.** Saruman

○ **B.** Radagast

○ **C.** Galadriel

○ **D.** All of the above

18. In the animated film, when Elrond reads the moon-letters, he actually recites the message on the map that in the book was already known to the dwarves.

○ **A.** True.

○ **B.** False.

19. In 2009, a partially completed manuscript co-written by Tolkien and C.S. Lewis was discovered in the Bodleian Library at Oxford University.

○ **A.** True.

○ **B.** False.

20. What film company originally owned the film rights to *The Hobbit*, but never capitalized on it with a movie?

○ **A.** New Line Cinema

○ **B.** Miramax

○ **C.** Universal

○ **D.** United Artists

21. How many Oscars did Peter Jackson's *The Lord of the Rings* trilogy win?

_____

welcome to hobbiton

After the filming of The Lord of the Rings, *the farm where Hobbiton was built remained open as a lucrative tourist attraction. When the production team returned to the farm for* The Hobbit, *the set was rebuilt in full, this time with more permanent fixtures, doors, hobbit-holes, and other details. Hobbiton remains a tourist attraction in Matamata, New Zealand, so even you can take a trip to the Shire.*

22. Who wrote and directed a children's theater adaptation of *The Hobbit*?

- **A.** Humphrey Carpenter
- **B.** Peter Jackson
- **C.** Robert Brustein
- **D.** Arvind Gaur

23. What Oscar-winning musician was an elf extra with a single line in the live-action version of *The Return of the King* and reprises his role in the *Hobbit* adaptations?

_____

24. In the live-action *The Hobbit*, Gloin makes his second appearance in a Peter Jackson adaptation of a Tolkien work, having attended the Council of Elrond in *The Fellowship of the Ring*.

- **A.** True.
- **B.** False.

25. This historically prominent film company went bankrupt in 2010, delaying filming of *The Hobbit*.

_____

26. *The Return of the King* is only the second sequel to ever win the Academy Award for Best Picture. What was the first?

_____

27. Christopher Lee and Ian Holm both returned to New Zealand to reprise their roles as Saruman and (Old) Bilbo Baggins for *The Hobbit*.

○ **A.** True.

○ **B.** False.

28. What is the name of the actor who played Gollum in *The Lord of the Rings* live-action films and King Kong in Jackson's remake, using motion-capture technology?

_____

29. *The Hobbit* films are not actually films—they were shot digitally.

○ **A.** True.

○ **B.** False.

30. Actor Martin Freeman, who plays Bilbo Baggins in *The Hobbit* films, has previously appeared in a movie in which Peter Jackson and Cate Blanchett appear. What is the film?

_____

31. After completing his lone scene in the film during the first week of shooting, Andy Serkis stayed on the live-action *The Hobbit* as the Second Unit Director.

○ **A.** True.

○ **B.** False.

32. In what BBC television show did live-action *The Hobbit* co-stars Martin Freeman (Bilbo) and Benedict Cumberbatch (Smaug) also co-star?

_____

33. *The Hobbit* and *The Lord of the Rings* were originally going to be produced as one film apiece.

○ **A.** True.

○ **B.** False.

speaking in Inglish

For the production of The Hobbit *text adventure game in 1982, programmer Stuart Richie developed an artificial intelligence system known as* Inglish. *It was considered revolutionary for the genre and for video games in general, as* Inglish *could understand and respond to a vast variety of words, commands, and sentence structures. While most "parsers" in games up until that time could only recognize limited verb-noun pairings,* Inglish *could also understand pronouns, adverbs, prepositions, and punctuation. Tolkien would surely be pleased to know his story led to the creation of yet another language.*

34. What actor was originally cast as Fili and even filmed several scenes before leaving the production for personal reasons?

○ **A.** John Krasinski

○ **B.** Rob Kazinsky

○ **C.** Dean O'Gorman

○ **D.** Richard Armitage

35. The actor who plays Gimli's father, Gloin, in *The Hobbit* is Gimli actor John Rhys-Davies's father, Jack Rhys, in real life.

○ **A.** True.

○ **B.** False.

36. Production company New Line Cinema struck a deal with a studio for the first time ever to distribute *The Hobbit* films. What is the studio?

_____

37. What is the official reason given for why Guillermo del Toro left the live-action film project?

   ○ **A.** Production delays

   ○ **B.** Peter Jackson decided he wanted to direct instead

   ○ **C.** Contract dispute

   ○ **D.** Health reasons

38. What organization issued a Do Not Work Order due to labor disputes related to *The Hobbit* production?

_____

39. How much money did the New Zealand government estimate it would have lost if *The Hobbit* were filmed in another country?

   ○ **A.** $500 million

   ○ **B.** $1 billion

   ○ **C.** $1.5 billion

   ○ **D.** $10 billion

40. Who said, "One of the drawbacks of *The Hobbit* is [that] it's relatively lightweight compared to *Lord of the Rings* . . ."?

_____

41. Jackson intended for The Hobbit to be as faithful to the book as possible.

   ○ **A.** True.

   ○ **B.** False.

48 Fps

Films are typically shot at 24 frames per second (fps). Even though they look "real," there is a subtle film-like quality that comes from the blur associated with a less-than-real frame rate. What the human eye sees is about the equivalent of 60 fps. For The Hobbit, director Peter Jackson decided to shoot at 48 fps, something that has rarely been done in cinema and was difficult to achieve before the advent of digital photography. The result is a heightened realism, and a blurred boundary between the movie and everyday life. Whether this aids the film or merely takes away some of its mystique, however, is in the eye of the beholder.

42. The budget of the three *Hobbit* films was more than the three *Lord of the Rings* films combined.

○ **A.** True.

○ **B.** False.

43. What was the estimated budget of each *Hobbit* live-action film?

_____

44. Which of these titles is *not* an expansion to *The Lord of the Rings Online: Shadows of Angmar*, the free, massively multiplayer online RPG?

○ **A.** Riders of Rohan

○ **B.** Mines of Moria

○ **C.** Rise of Isengard

○ **D.** Battle for Minas Tirith

45. Because he left the project, Guillermo del Toro did not receive a screenwriting credit for his contributions to *The Hobbit* live-action movie.

○ **A.** True.

○ **B.** False.

46. What game studio developed the original *The Hobbit* video game in 1982?

_____

47. A copy of the book was included with every copy of the 1982 *The Hobbit* video game.

○ **A.** True.

○ **B.** False.

48. What is the name of *The Hobbit* parody game, released by CRL in 1986?

_____

49. What kind of video game was *The Hobbit* (1982)?

_____

50. What game studio released a platform video game version of *The Hobbit* in 2003, at the height of *The Lord of the Rings*'s popularity?

_____

The Missing Hobbit

Sometime in the 1970s, the master tapes of the 1968 BBC series of The Hobbit were wiped. It's true that this was common practice for the space-consuming tapes of the time, but in this case it was rumored that they had been wiped due to a dispute with the Tolkien Estate. The BBC eventually recovered an off-air FM recording that had been stitched together from the original broadcast. They re-edited the tapes back into thirty-minute episodes and eventually sold the series commercially, indicating that if there were ever a dispute with the Tolkien Estate, it had been resolved.

51. For what 2011 film was *The Lord of the Rings* and *The Hobbit* composer nominated for an Oscar for Best Original Score?

_____

52. The composer for Peter Jackson's *Lord of the Rings* and *The Hobbit* films spent five years early in his career as a music director on which show?

   ○ **A.** *Saturday Night Live*

   ○ **B.** *Taxi*

   ○ **C.** *The Wonder Years*

   ○ **D.** *Sesame Street*

53. Who is the composer who won three Oscars for his work on *The Lord of the Rings* and returned to work with Peter Jackson on *The Hobbit*?

_____

54. Ian McKellen is the only actor playing a member of Thorin's party who does not have to wear prosthetics.

○ **A.** True.

○ **B.** False.

55. For how many days did the live-action *The Hobbit* shoot?

○ **A.** 87

○ **B.** 100

○ **C.** 143

○ **D.** 254

56. What is the name of the London studio where some of the live-action *The Hobbit* was shot (the only shooting location outside of New Zealand)?

_____

57. For what reason did Peter Jackson say he dreaded making *The Hobbit*?

○ **A.** Not enough money

○ **B.** He was bored of the universe

○ **C.** Too many dwarves

○ **D.** Exhaustion

FIGWIT

In The Return of the King *extended edition, there is a scene in which Arwen makes the decision to stay in Middle-earth and leaves the procession of elves to the Havens. Then-unknown actor, Bret McKenzie, who went on to star in the comedy show* The Flight of the Conchords, *played the elf who (futilely) implored Arwen to stay. In the credits he is referred to only as "Elf Escort," but an online community of fans bestowed upon him the endearing nickname Figwit. He became so popular among fans that Peter Jackson invited him back to appear in* The Hobbit, *but this time gave him a real Elvish name: Lindir.*

58. To achieve the illusion of small dwarves and hobbits, each actor has a much shorter body double in full costume and makeup.

- ○ **A.** True.
- ○ **B.** False.

59. *The Hobbit* live-action films were shot in 3-D.

- ○ **A.** True.
- ○ **B.** False.

60. How many cameras were used to shoot the live-action *The Hobbit?*

- ○ **A.** 2
- ○ **B.** 8
- ○ **C.** 12
- ○ **D.** 16

61. Peter Jackson named all of the cameras used on *The Hobbit*. Which of the following did he *not* name any cameras after?

○ **A.** The dwarves

○ **B.** Family members

○ **C.** Pets

○ **D.** The Beatles

62. There were two concept designers working on Peter Jackson's *The Hobbit* so that the sketches could be seen in 3-D.

○ **A.** True.

○ **B.** False.

63. Jackson ordered the set for Mirkwood to be painted with bright, psychedelic colors. What was the reason?

○ **A.** To illustrate the effects of the spider poison

○ **B.** Because after film processing and color correction, the colors look much more tame

○ **C.** Because this is how Tolkien describes it

○ **D.** To illustrate the effects of the black river

The hobbit in 3-D

Peter Jackson is an outspoken advocate of 3-D films. In one of his production diaries leading up to the release of The Hobbit, *Jackson said, "If I had the ability to shoot* Lord of the Rings *in 3-D, I certainly would have done it." Even though the craze hadn't yet caught on at the turn of the millennium, Jackson took his own 3-D still photographs on the set of the original trilogy. If he has his way, one day the photos will be released as a bonus feature on a 3-D Blu-Ray special edition of the films.*

64. For Jackson's films of *The Hobbit,* in order to make the dwarves' skin look natural on camera, makeup artists added heightened levels of blue to their makeup.

○ **A.** True.

○ **B.** False.

65. What is the name of the Wellington, New Zealand, studios at which Jackson filmed *The Hobbit?*

_____

66. What kind of ceremony was held to celebrate the start of production for Peter Jackson's *The Hobbit?*

○ **A.** A traditional christening

○ **B.** The reciting of an elvish blessing

○ **C.** A wedding between two *Lord of the Rings* crew members

○ **D.** A Powhiri welcoming ceremony

67. What school performed the first stage play adaptation of *The Hobbit?*

○ **A.** St. Margaret's School, Edinburgh

○ **B.** Oxford University

○ **C.** Pembroke College

○ **D.** Julliard School

68. What BBC radio channel aired a voice-acted adaptation of *The Hobbit* in eight half-hour episodes?

_____

fULL-cOLOR fILm

William L. Snyder, an American film producer, obtained the rights to The Hobbit *while it was still relatively unknown and therefore cheap. However, as part of the deal he was obligated to make a "full-color film" by June 30, 1966, in order to retain the rights. His feature-length project never got off the ground, but soon the book had. Snyder then realized that "full-color" didn't specify a length, and he produced a twelve-minute animated film. It was called* The Hobbit!*—with an exclamation point, presumably because he was so pleased about being able to sell the film rights to the now immensely popular book.*

69. The BBC radio adaptation referred to in Question 68 added an additional narrator to the tale called the "Tale Bearer."

○ **A.** True.

○ **B.** False.

70. The master recordings of the BBC radio broadcast were lost in a studio fire in 1973.

○ **A.** True.

○ **B.** False.

71. The production of the BBC radio series was routinely delayed due to the labor-intensive sound mixing and effects recording needed for each episode.

○ **A.** True.

○ **B.** False.

72. The 1968 BBC radio series was based on the original, first edition of *The Hobbit*.

   ○ **A.** True.

   ○ **B.** False.

73. In 1972, an off-Broadway musical of *The Hobbit* hit the stage. What other musical earned lyricist David Rogers a Tony?

_____

74. In *The Hobbit—A Musical*, the elvish swords were made to glow by wiring fluorescent tube lights inside the props.

   ○ **A.** True.

   ○ **B.** False.

75. In the Argo Records audio release of *The Hobbit* in 1974, what actor played more than twenty different characters, each with a different voice?

_____

76. What actor from *The Fellowship of the Ring* (2001) played Frodo in the 1981 BBC radio adaptation of *The Lord of the Rings*?

_____

77. The animation team behind *The Hobbit* also made an animated version of *The Return of the King* to patch up things left out of Ralph Bakshi's 1978 *The Lord of the Rings*.

O **A.** True.

O **B.** False.

78. This actor voiced Bilbo in the animated version of *The Hobbit*, as well as Frodo and old Bilbo in the animated *The Return of the King*.

_____

79. What BBC children's television series created an adaptation of *The Hobbit* but supposedly had its video release halted repeatedly by the Tolkien Estate?

_____

80. What musician spent much of the 1970s writing a two-part opera based on *The Hobbit*?

_____

81. The two halves of *The Hobbit* opera were named after these two chapters from the book.

_____

82. The 1977 version of *The Hobbit* is the first animated adaptation of the book.

○ **A.** True.

○ **B.** False.

83. What director did William L. Snyder enlist to write and direct an adaptation of *The Hobbit* in order to retain his rights to the property?

_____

84. During the Cold War, *The Hobbit* and *The Lord of the Rings* were banned from Soviet Russia.

○ **A.** True.

○ **B.** False.

85. At one point in the late sixties, the Beatles planned to do a *Lord of the Rings* film. Match the Beatle to the character they reportedly would have played.

A. John Lennon   **i.** Sam

B. Paul McCartney   **ii.** Frodo

C. George Harrison   **iii.** Gandalf

D. Ringo Starr   **iv.** Gollum

86. Stanley Kubrick turned down the opportunity to direct *The Lord of the Rings* because he thought the trilogy was too big to be filmed.

○ **A.** True.

○ **B.** False.

87. In 2009, a fan film was made based on Aragorn's search for Gollum, a tale told briefly in *The Hunt for the Ring* in *Unfinished Tales*. What was it called?

_____

88. Disney at one point held the rights to *The Hobbit*, but never made a film because they could not generate a script to Tolkien's liking.

○ **A.** True.

○ **B.** False.

89. What is the name of the 1993 Finnish TV miniseries that tells the story of both *The Hobbit* and *The Lord of the Rings*?

_____

90. In 1972, Dramatic Publishing released *The Hobbit: A Musical*. In it, several names of enemies and secondary characters were changed. Most notably, Elrond has become an elf-queen. What is her name?

_____

91. Being notably shorter, the musical's elf-queen seems to account for both Elrond and the Elvenking. Whom does she call upon to get Thorin's party quickly to the "Great Mountain"?

_____

92. In the musical version of *The Hobbit*, Bilbo kills Smaug (who is in this version named "Smowg").

○ **A.** True.

○ **B.** False

93. With music from Aulis Sallinen, Marjo Kuusela produced a *Hobbit* ballet in 2001 called *Hobitti*. In what country was this made?

_____

94. In the 2003 video game adaptation of *The Hobbit*, who is the only playable character?

_____

95. The Best Original Soundtrack of the Year winner at the Game Developer's Conference in 2004, *The Hobbit* adventure game was scored by the same composer as Jackson's *Lord of the Rings* films.

○ **A.** True.

○ **B.** False.

96. What game publisher issued two board games based on *The Hobbit*?

_____

Chapter 6 Answer Key

1.	South Park.
2.	D.
3.	John Huston.
4.	B.
5.	Horns.
6.	Six.
7.	Japan.
8.	True.
9.	True.
10.	Guillermo del Toro.
11.	An Unexpected Journey & There and Back Again.
12.	Ian McKellen.
13.	True.
14.	False. It is the only song in the movie not written by Tolkien for the book.
15.	Beorn.
16.	Tauriel.
17.	D.
18.	True.
19.	True.
20.	D.
21.	Seventeen.
22.	A.
23.	Bret McKenzie.
24.	True.
25.	MGM.
26.	*The Godfather Part II.*
27.	False. They both reprised their roles but filmed their scenes in England due to health concerns related to traveling to New Zealand.
28.	Andy Serkis.
29.	True.
30.	*Hot Fuzz.*
31.	True.
32.	*Sherlock.*
33.	False. *The Lord of the Rings* was originally going to be two films, and *The Hobbit* a single film.
34.	B.
35.	False.
36.	20th Century Fox.
37.	D.
38.	International Federation of Actors.
39.	C.
40.	Peter Jackson.
41.	False. He wanted to explore gaps in the tale and better connect them to his previous Tolkien films.
42.	True.
43.	$150 million.
44.	D.
45.	False.
46.	Beam.
47.	True.
48.	The Boggit.
49.	Text adventure.
50.	Vivendi Universal.

51.	*Hugo*.	78.	Orson Bean.
52.	A.	79.	Jackanory.
53.	Howard Shore.	80.	Paul Corfield Godfrey.
54.	False. Ian McKellen wears a prosthetic nose, as well as false eyebrows and a wig.	81.	"Over Hill and Under Hill" and "Fire and Water."
55.	D.	82.	False.
56.	Pinewood Studios.	83.	Gene Deitch.
57.	C.	84.	False. There was a Soviet television play called "The Adventure of the Hobbit" made in 1985.
58.	True.	85.	A-iv, B-ii, C-iii, D-i.
59.	True.	86.	True.
60.	D.	87.	*The Hunt for Gollum*.
61.	A.	88.	False. Disney never held the rights to any of Tolkien's work.
62.	True.	89.	*Hobitit*.
63.	B.	90.	Elfrida.
64.	False. They added heightened levels of red.	91.	The King of the Eagles.
65.	Stone Street Studios.	92.	True.
66.	D.	93.	Finland.
67.	A.	94.	Bilbo.
68.	Radio 4.	95.	False.
69.	True.	96.	Fantasy Flight Games.
70.	False. They were intentionally wiped.		
71.	False. The sound effects were added live.		
72.	False. It was based on the revised 1951 version.		
73.	*Charlie and Algernon*.		
74.	False. They used glow-in-the-dark paint and black lights.		
75.	Nicol Williamson.		
76.	Ian Holm.		
77.	True.		

Score Your Adaptation Erudition!

In this section, there are 99 possible right answers.

If you got 0–34 right, you should know that there's a whole world of entertainment out there. It's about time you checked it out.

If you got 35–65 right, then we're guessing you're a "Who needs the special edition, I'm never going to watch all that junk anyway," kind of fan.

If you got 66–99 right, you should consider becoming a serious critic. Movies, music, food? Why not all three?

CHAPTER 7

CREATORS

Growing and maintaining a mythical world is hard work. Think of it like gardening, only replace all the dirt with strained eyeballs, the fertilizer with tired brains, and the shovel with carpal tunnel syndrome.

For Tolkien, the craft came first. To himself he was a father telling bedtime stories more than he was a professor studying and lecturing on Norse poetry and linguistics. And he was a professor more than he was an author. And he was certainly an author more than he was the father of modern fantasy. Perhaps this is why he didn't write more books: "Why," he might have asked himself, "should I hop around and waste precious time creating new worlds when everything I could ever want to create is possible right here in Middle-earth."

Many others have thought the same. Entire careers have been built from Tolkien's imagination: from academics, to artists and other authors, all the way up to Peter Jackson. If Tolkien is the Bilbo of his own tale, then perhaps Jackson is the Aragorn. Well, not physically, but just consider his role. He came in from relative obscurity—from dark places, mostly—then reclaimed a great land and improved upon it. Sure, Middle-earth probably would have survived without him, but it was crying out for a leader—even as it was cautioning lesser souls that turning some of the most beloved books of the past century into films was something that could not be done.

So now that Tolkien has sailed across the sea to the Undying Lands, he can rest easily knowing that Middle-earth has its king.

1. What does the J.R.R. in J.R.R. Tolkien stand for?

   _____

2. Tolkien provided his own illustrations for the English and
   American publications of *The Hobbit.*

   ○ **A.** True.

   ○ **B.** False.

3. On what did Tolkien say he originally wrote the famous first line,
   "In a hole in the ground there lived a hobbit"?

   _____

4. What was Tolkien's preferred means of writing?

   _____

5. Tolkien loathed all things Disney.

   ○ **A.** True.

   ○ **B.** False.

6. Like Bilbo, Tolkien's grandfather was well respected and his
   mother was one of three daughters.

   ○ **A.** True.

   ○ **B.** False.

7. The party's trek through the mountains was based on Tolkien's own journey through what country in 1911?

_____

8. What was Tolkien's favorite color of dragon, which gets special treatment in _The Hobbit_?

_____

9. Prior to becoming a renowned fantasy author, Tolkien was a compiler for the _Merriam-Webster Dictionary._

○ **A.** True.

○ **B.** False.

10. Which of Tolkien's children devoted most of his life to editing and organizing his father's many writings related to the histories, languages, and details of Middle-earth?

_____

11. When they were young, Tolkien would write his children letters from fictional characters every year for what holiday?

_____

12. When was J.R.R. Tolkien born?

_____

BEOWULF AND TOLKIEN

"Beowulf: The Monster and the Critics," a lecture given by Tolkien in 1936, is one of his best-known pieces of literary criticism. Its subject, the poem Beowulf, is also one of the best-known (though not necessarily the most widely read today) works of Anglo-Saxon literature. It's somewhat astonishing, then, to realize that it comes to us hanging on by the slenderest of threads.

The poem exists in a single manuscript, dating to the late-tenth or early-eleventh century. Although some internal evidence suggests the poet was a Christian, scholars have also argued that the "Christian" passages were later interpolations by another writer.

The general consensus is that the events of the poem take place around the fifth century, and that the story was probably oral in its original form and only written down much later.

Many elements of the story had a profound influence on Tolkien's world, including dragons attacked by heroes, a great mead-hall (strongly resembling Edoras, the seat of Théoden of Rohan), and the alliterative form of the poem, which Tolkien imitated in his "translation" of the poetry of the Rohirrim in The Lord of the Rings.

13. Tolkien never published a fiction book outside of the Middle-earth universe.

○ **A.** True.

○ **B.** False.

14. Which of the following is *not* a Tolkien story?

○ **A.** *Mr. Bliss*

○ **B.** *Roverandom*

○ **C.** *Farmer Giles of Ham*

○ **D.** *On Goblin-Tales*

15. While working as a dictionary compiler, Tolkien primarily worked on words beginning with what letter?

○ **A.** C

○ **B.** G

○ **C.** S

○ **D.** W

16. Tolkien was strongly opposed to the idea of a dramatic adaptation of his work.

○ **A.** True.

○ **B.** False.

17. Tolkien completed *The Hobbit* and *The Lord of the Rings* entirely at one desk.

○ **A.** True.

○ **B.** False.

18. Which of Tolkien's major works was published posthumously?

_____

19. Which animal's name's origin proved difficult to ascertain during Tolkien's time as a dictionary compiler?

○ **A.** Horse

○ **B.** Walrus

○ **C.** Thrush

○ **D.** Bee

20.   Where did Tolkien begin his formal education?

_____

21.   What was the name of the literary club to which Tolkien belonged from the 1930s to the 1940s?

_____

22.   What is the name of the famed Oxford pub where the club referred to in Question 21 would hold its meetings?

_____

23.   Why did Tolkien originally begin writing _The Hobbit_?

○   **A.** For a class

○   **B.** For his children

○   **C.** He was encouraged by a friend

○   **D.** To get published

24.   After the publication of _The Lord of the Rings_, Tolkien vowed that he would never again return to the text of _The Hobbit_.

○   **A.** True.

○   **B.** False.

TOLKIEN AND "JACK" LEWIS

Tolkien's relationship to C.S. Lewis was a complicated one and deeply important to both men. They met at Oxford, when "Jack" Lewis took the opposite side in a dispute within the English faculty at Merton College. Tolkien believed in a strong emphasis on ancient languages, and resented the presence in the curriculum of anything so modern as Shakespeare. Lewis took what today we would think of as a more modern approach.

Despite this, the two became firm friends and colleagues, first as members of the "Coalbiter's Society" and later as members of the Inklings. Tolkien played a key role in turning Lewis away from agnosticism back toward Christianity. However, Lewis became an Anglican and Tolkien, as a member of the Roman Catholic faith, rather resented this.

The men also differed in their love of fantasy. While Lewis liked The Hobbit *and those bits of* The Lord of the Rings *and* The Silmarillion *that Tolkien read to the Inklings, Tolkien strongly disliked his friend's Narnia stories. He thought them childish and lacking the high seriousness of his own fantasy.*

Tolkien also strongly disapproved of Lewis's marriage to the American Joy Davidman Gresham, and this widened the growing breach between the men. Although they remained on friendly terms, their relationship did not have the same warmth as in earlier days.

25. What is the title of the film, other than *The Lord of the Rings* movies, for which Peter Jackson and his wife were nominated for an Oscar for Best Original Screenplay?

_____

26. Tolkien was only married once, for the rest of his life. What was his wife's name?

_____

27. Tolkien had a PhD in linguistics.

   ○ **A.** True.

   ○ **B.** False.

28. Fill in the blank: Tolkien was a very religious man, a devout

_____ .

29. Tolkien was opposed to overt religious allegory in stories.

   ○ **A.** True.

   ○ **B.** False.

30. What name did Tolkien have engraved on his wife's tombstone after a beautiful immortal from his own ancient Middle-earth lore?

_____

31. Tolkien served as a code-breaker for Britain during World War II.

   ○ **A.** True.

   ○ **B.** False.

32. By what university was Tolkien employed while he wrote *The Hobbit*?

_____

33. Tolkien was bitten by a tarantula as a child in South Africa.

    ○ **A.** True.

    ○ **B.** False.

34. What other film had Peter Jackson asked Guillermo del Toro to direct prior to *The Hobbit*?

    ○ **A.** *The Return of the King*

    ○ **B.** *King Kong*

    ○ **C.** *Halo*

    ○ **D.** *The Lovely Bones*

35. In 2009, this low-budget sci-fi film set in South Africa unexpectedly earned Jackson his fourth Best Picture nomination.

_____

36. What surgery did Jackson receive that delayed the production of *The Hobbit*?

    ○ **A.** Heart

    ○ **B.** Perforated ulcer

    ○ **C.** Stomach reduction

    ○ **D.** Bunion

37. What is the name of Peter Jackson's longtime writing and producing partner, who also happens to be his wife?

_____

38. Peter Jackson saw Ralph Bakshi's animated films before he ever read *The Lord of the Rings.*

○ **A.** True.

○ **B.** False

39. What film was Peter Jackson offered to direct and originally set to film before *The Lord of the Rings?*

○ **A.** *The Hobbit*

○ **B.** *King Kong*

○ **C.** *The Lovely Bones*

○ **D.** *Halo*

40. Peter Jackson sued New Line Cinema in 2005. Why?

○ **A.** They would not give him several of his Oscars

○ **B.** They were contractually obligated to him, but offered *The Hobbit* to another director

○ **C.** To request an audit so that he could ensure he had been paid enough money from *The Lord of the Rings* earnings

○ **D.** New Line had misused Jackson's previous films as promotional materials without permission

41. The Tolkien Trust also sued New Line Cinema for the same reason as in Question 40.

○ **A.** True.

○ **B.** False.

42. Peter Jackson has a large collection of World War II memorabilia.

　　○ **A.** True.

　　○ **B.** False.

43. To what kind of research did Jackson and Walsh contribute $311,000 to the University of California?

　　○ **A.** Cancer

　　○ **B.** Stem cell

　　○ **C.** Cloning

　　○ **D.** Space travel

44. On what continent was Tolkien born?

_____

45. When Great Britain entered the Great War (World War I), Tolkien immediately enlisted in the British Army.

　　○ **A.** True.

　　○ **B.** False.

46. What is the name of Jackson's aircraft restoration company?

_____

A hobbit's hole

One author who was a favorite of Tolkien's—as well as of millions of others—was the children's writer Kenneth Grahame, best known for his classic The Wind in the Willows. If we go looking for sources for Tolkien's descriptions of Mr. Baggins's home, we might start with this book.

Three of the four chief characters in Grahame's tale, the Mole, the Water Rat, and the Badger, live underground. Toad Hall, residence of Mr. Toad, is magnificent but less homelike and comfortable than the other three, a fact that's remarked on several times. The Mole—the chief character for the first half of the book—in fact feels more at home underground and remarks as much to the Badger. "Once well underground," he observes, "you know exactly where you are. Nothing can happen to you, and nothing can get at you. You're entirely your own master . . . Things go on all the same overhead, and you let 'em, and don't bother about 'em. When you want to, up you go, and there the things are, waiting for you." That might serve as a succinct summary of Bilbo's philosophy.

Badger, who lives in a rambling underground house, excavated on the ruins of a once-great city, heartily agrees. Even Rat, who prefers the fresh air of the river blowing on his face whenever possible, lives in a snug hole in the river bank, including a parlor with a fireplace, pleasant bedrooms, and the usual domestic accoutrements.

Hobbits, as becomes clearer in The Lord of the Rings, dislike high places and feel most comfortable underground. This explains why some of Bilbo's most traumatic moments during his adventure happen in high spots: in the mountains during the storm; at the top of a fir tree (with goblins and wolves gathered below); and in the eyrie of an eagle.

In Frodo's time, the hobbits of the Shire build houses, but they're generally one story and rounded to resemble hobbit-holes. Actual hobbit-holes, Tolkien makes clear, were growing more rare and were inhabited by either very wealthy hobbits (as was the case with Bilbo) or very poor ones, who dug a hasty tunnel in a sandbank and moved in.

47. In 2006, Jackson partnered with Microsoft Game Studios and formed a new company to make film-caliber video games. What was the name of the company?

_____

48. Tolkien recalls that the first story he ever wrote, at age seven, concerned this type of beast, which features prominently in *The Hobbit*.

_____

49. Tolkien was one of the founders of the Oxford Order of the Catenian Association, a religious group devoted to Catholicism. What was his elected role in the association?

_____

50. Like Frodo, Tolkien lost both of his parents at a very young age (though, unlike Frodo, not both at once).

○ **A.** True.

○ **B.** False.

51. Tolkien met his future wife when he was sixteen (she was nineteen), but was forbidden to see her until she was twenty-one by his guardian. Before communication ceased, he proposed.

○ **A.** True.

○ **B.** False.

52. This apostle, said to be Tolkien's "favorite," is typically depicted as an eagle and is considered an inspiration to his great eagle lords.

_____

53. Tolkien considered his favorite book as a child Lewis Carroll's *Through the Looking Glass.*

○ **A.** True.

○ **B.** False.

54. Tolkien had only one sibling, a younger sister named Hilary.

○ **A.** True.

○ **B.** False.

55. Tolkien considered himself a hobbit, excepting one crucial factor. What was it?

○ **A.** Laziness

○ **B.** Size

○ **C.** Hairy feet

○ **D.** Appetite

56. Tolkien fought in a famous World War I battle, after which he returned home with trench sickness. What was the name of the battle?

_____

57. Though his mother died of diabetes in 1904, Tolkien believed that it was her family's opposition to her conversion to Roman Catholicism that accelerated her death.

○ **A.** True.

○ **B.** False.

58. Tolkien's mother left him in the care of a priest at a Roman Catholic parish in Birmingham, England. What was his name?

_____

59. Tolkien's guardian disapproved of and forbade the young love between him and Edith, similar to the disapproval of what king in the story of Beren and Lúthien in *The Silmarillion*?

_____

60. Though he is known the world over as J.R.R. Tolkien, what name did he go by with friends and family?

_____

61. What is the original name of Jackson's 1992 "splatstick" film, renamed *Dead Alive* for North American release?

_____

62. Despite being a New Zealand citizen, Peter Jackson was knighted by the Queen of England in 2010 for his work on *The Lord of the Rings* and for his philanthropy.

○ **A.** True.

○ **B.** False.

63. What film, which Jackson attempted to recreate using his own stop-motion models and a Super 8 camera as a child, does he consider his all-time favorite?

_____

64. What is the name of Jackson's first feature film, in which he famously fights himself atop a cliff?

_____

65. Due to his environmentalist beliefs, Tolkien never owned a car.

○ **A.** True.

○ **B.** False.

66. As a young boy, Tolkien was once chased by a farmer for picking his mushrooms, whom he nicknamed the Black Ogre.

○ **A.** True.

○ **B.** False.

67. Like the dwarves and elves of Middle-earth, Tolkien was very musically inclined, his second great passion in youth after linguistics.

O **A.** True.

O **B.** False.

68. In the town where Tolkien grew up, there was a Dr. Gamgee, who invented something called . . . a gamgee. What was it?

_____

69. Tolkien's aunt, May Suffield, traveled home to England from South Africa when she heard her sister, Tolkien's mother, was becoming a Roman Catholic.

O **A.** True.

O **B.** False.

70. Concerned about the creative direction of proposed film adaptations of his work in his lifetime, Tolkien divided the rights to *The Hobbit* and *The Lord of the Rings* equally among his children.

O **A.** True.

O **B.** False.

71. Before the release of *The Fellowship of the Ring*, Christopher Tolkien said publicly that *The Lord of the Rings* were unsuitable for transformation into dramatic visual form.

O **A.** True.

O **B.** False.

72. In 2007, Tolkien's final original work was released, a story he began as early as 1918 and brought to near completion in the 1950s but never finished. What is the title of this work?

_____

73. Including Elvish in its various incarnations and dialects, Tolkien created more than twenty languages in his lifetime.

○ **A.** True.

○ **B.** False.

74. Which of the following was *not* one of the Middle English poems Tolkien translated?

○ **A.** *The Pearl*

○ **B.** *Sir Gawain and the Green Knight*

○ **C.** *Sir Orfeo*

○ **D.** *Gentilesse*

75. After her engagement to Tolkien, Edith converted to Roman Catholicism much to his delight. Her Protestant landlord, however, was less pleased: He kicked her out of her home.

○ **A.** True.

○ **B.** False.

76. How was Edith able to communicate with her husband and track his movements in the trenches of World War I?

○ **A.** They developed a coded letter writing system, which only they could decode

○ **B.** Tolkien befriended his battalion's telegram operator

○ **C.** She was not able to—much to her dismay

○ **D.** Tolkien ignored the army's postal censorship and several letters slipped through

77. Endearingly, Tolkien would often refer to his wife as Lúthien.

○ **A.** True.

○ **B.** False.

78. The publication of *The Lord of the Rings* was delayed for over a year after its completion due to the royalties issues.

○ **A.** True.

○ **B.** False.

79. This co-director of *The Hobbit* animated feature went on to write children's books himself, including a series starring Herb the Vegetarian Dragon.

_____

80. Screenwriter Romeo Muller won an award for his teleplay of *The Hobbit*. What was the award?

   ○ **A.** Emmy

   ○ **B.** Peabody Award

   ○ **C.** Hugo Award

   ○ **D.** Newberry Award

81. Who was Tolkien's illustrator of choice, the illustrator of several maps of Middle-earth, as well as covers of many of Tolkien's other children's books?

_____

82. Tolkien was visiting publisher Allen & Unwin to complain about the illustrations for his upcoming novella when he saw spec work that had been sent in by the illustrator referred to in Question 81 and demanded she be hired immediately. What was the project, their very first collaboration?

_____

83. Perhaps the second most famous fantasy series of the twentieth century was written by Tolkien's best friend and fellow literary club founder. What is the name of the series?

_____

84. What is the name of the UK society that was founded in 1969 "to further interest in the life and works of J.R.R. Tolkien"?

---

85. Into what country was Tolkien deployed in World War I?

---

86. In addition to length, Tolkien's publishers rejected *The Silmarillion* because they found the names and stories "too Celtic."

○ **A.** True.

○ **B.** False.

87. This artist, who has painted a great number of Tolkien-inspired illustrations, including of *The Hobbit,* was commissioned by Christopher Tolkien to help create a fully illustrated version of *The Silmarillion*, which was released in 1998.

---

88. Before becoming a Professor of English Language and Literature in 1945, what was Tolkien a professor of for twenty years?

---

89. In 2003, The Tolkien Society began the Tolkien Reading Day, an annual day for old fans and new to read and appreciate Tolkien's stories. On what day is it observed?

_____

90. In 1967, a British composer produced a song cycle based on *The Hobbit* and *The Lord of the Rings* named after Bilbo's famous poem, "The Road Goes Ever On." Who is the composer?

_____

91. Though he was a religious man, many of the poems and myths that inspired Tolkien were inspired by the constellations and stars. What's Tolkien's sign?

_____

92. *The Hobbit*'s Oscar-winning director of photography has also shot sci-fi hits *I Am Legend* and *King Kong* (though less notably, *The Last Airbender*). Who is he?

_____

93. Jackson's wife, Fran Walsh, has contributed to all of his feature films but one. Which one did she miss?

_____

94. How many children do Jackson and Walsh have together?

_____

95. What screenwriter, whose first film writing credits were on *The Lord of the Rings* trilogy with Jackson and Walsh, returned to cowrite the *Hobbit* films as well?

_____

96. Prior to forming the Inklings, Tolkien and Lewis belonged to a society dedicated to reading Icelandic sagas. What was its name?

_____

97. What was the origin of the name of the society referred to in Question 96?

_____

98. In 1993, a film was made focusing on the aging C.S. Lewis and his relationship with a young American poet. What was the name of the film?

_____

99. Although the Inklings involved a number of different writers, Tolkien and Lewis are most often mentioned in it, along with a third writer. What is his name?

_____

100. What was the first university at which Tolkien taught?

_____

101. Scholars at Oxford in the Honour School of Language and Literature had argued since the school's founding about whether the English course offered at the university should consist of a study of ancient and medieval texts, stopping at Chaucer, or whether it should include everything up to modern literature. Which side did Tolkien take in this debate?

_____

102. What important literary critic referred to *The Lord of the Rings* as "an overgrown fairy story, a philological curiosity"?

_____

103. What nineteenth-century artist and fantasist strongly influenced Tolkien both in his art and in his writing?

_____

Chapter 7 Answer Key

1.	John Ronald Reuel.	27.	False. But he was rewarded an honorary Doctorate of Letters from the University of Oxford.
2.	True.		
3.	On the back of a student's exam booklet.	28.	Roman Catholic.
4.	Typewriter.	29.	True. Though he himself was deeply religious.
5.	True.	30.	Lúthien.
6.	True.	31.	False. He was earmarked to become one, but his services were never required.
7.	Switzerland.		
8.	Green.	32.	University of Oxford.
9.	False. He was a compiler for the Oxford English Dictionary.	33.	True.
		34.	C.
10.	Christopher Tolkien.	35.	*District 9.*
11.	Christmas.	36.	B.
12.	January 3, 1892.	37.	Fran Walsh.
13.	False.	38.	True.
14.	D.	39.	B.
15.	D.	40.	C.
16.	False. He sold the film, stage, and merchandising rights to United Artists in 1968.	41.	True.
		42.	False. It is World War I memorabilia.
17.	True.	43.	B.
18.	*The Silmarillion.*	44.	Africa.
19.	B.	45.	False. He entered a program that allowed him to delay enlistment until after he completed his degree.
20.	King Edward's School.		
21.	The Inklings.	46.	The Vintage Aviator.
22.	The Eagle and Child.	47.	Wingnut Interactive.
23.	B.	48.	A dragon.
24.	False. He attempted to re-envision it in 1960 but never completed it.	49.	Vice President.
		50.	True.
25.	*Heavenly Creatures.*	51.	False. Tolkien wrote her a letter on her twenty-first birthday asking for her hand in marriage.
26.	Edith.		

52.	John the Evangelist.		76.	A.
53.	False. His favorite was S.R. Crockett's *The Black Douglas*, though he held Carroll in very high regard.		77.	False. Though he did draw the connection internally, especially after her death.
54.	False. He indeed had a sibling named Hilary but this was his younger brother.		78.	False.
			79.	Jules Bass.
55.	B.		80.	B.
56.	The Battle of the Somme.		81.	Pauline Baynes.
57.	True.		82.	*Farmer Giles of Ham.*
58.	Father Francis Morgan.		83.	The Chronicles of Narnia.
59.	King Thingol.		84.	The Tolkien Society.
60.	Ronald.		85.	France.
61.	*Braindead.*		86.	True.
62.	False. Jackson was knighted, however, in his native New Zealand.		87.	Ted Nasmith.
63.	*King Kong.*		88.	Anglo-Saxon.
64.	*Bad Taste.*		89.	March 25.
65.	False. He bought a Morris Cowley in 1932.		90.	Donald Swann.
66.	True.		91.	Capricorn. Though asking him probably wouldn't have scored you a date.
67.	False. He had little interest or knack for playing music, though he did enjoy it (as is evident from his many songs).		92.	Andrew Lesnie.
68.	A cotton wool tissue used for surgical dressing.		93.	*Bad Taste.*
			94.	Two.
69.	False. May and Mabel, curiously, decided to convert to Catholicism concurrently, without knowing that the other was converting as well. They were a continent apart.		95.	Philippa Boyens.
			96.	The Coalbiter's Society.
70.	False. Tolkien sold the film rights in 1969.		97.	It came from the Old Icelandic *Kolbítar,* referring to men who sat so close to the fire that they "bit the coal."
71.	True.			
72.	*The Children of Húrin.*		98.	*Shadowlands.*
73.	True.		99.	Charles Williams.
74.	D.		100.	Leeds University, where he was appointed a Reader in English Language.
75.	True.			

101.	He argued strongly for the first position.
102.	Edmund Wilson.
103.	William Morris.

Score Your Creator Comprehension!

In this section, there are 103 possible right answers.

If you got 0–34 right, you've got the blacksmith skills of an orc. A few clever things, but certainly no beautiful things.

If you got 35–65 right, you've got the forgery skills of men. Maybe not as flashy as the elves, but they pack a wallop.

If you got 66–103 right, you're a master blacksmith. Feel free to form up with the dwarves or the elves—surely either would be happy to have you in their ranks.

CHAPTER 8

MIDDLE-EARTH AND BEYOND

Perhaps J.R.R. Tolkien's greatest success as an author is not the epic story he tells, but the world he created. As robust as the characters are in *The Hobbit* and *The Lord of the Rings*, one of the most exciting aspects of his books is the larger world they suggest: a full world, with its own sprawling history, changing landscapes, diverse languages, taxonomies, races, creeds, religions, trajectories, and beliefs. In fact, the world of Middle-earth is so vast and complex that it could not be contained in a single lifetime.

Tolkien's youngest son, Christopher, spent most of his life organizing and filling in the expansive details of Middle-earth, like his father before him. Everything from the great wars of history to the color of a particular character's hat was examined by Christopher. Even after *The Lord of the Rings* was first published in 1955, Tolkien spent the remainder of his life trying to achieve a vision nearly impossible in scope—a full, breathing, living world, with no limit of stories to tell.

He drew maps and family trees, and did his best to reconcile *The Hobbit*, which began as a mere hobby, with *The Lord of the Rings*, the book that many would agree is his true masterpiece (though opinion among Tolkienists is somewhat divided on that topic). It would take a lifetime of scholarly effort to truly grasp it all, but surely that's something you can spare time for. Let's see how you're doing, shall we?

1. What popular toy released a *Lord of the Rings* line for the first time in its long history in the summer of 2012, in anticipation of the *Hobbit* films?

_____

2. Where is the upscale restaurant known as "The Hobbit" located?

  ○ **A.** Oxford, England

  ○ **B.** Orange, California

  ○ **C.** Matamata, New Zealand

  ○ **D.** New York, New York

3. For what feature is The Hobbit restaurant renowned?

  ○ **A.** Its wine cellar

  ○ **B.** It is built into a hill like a hobbit-hole

  ○ **C.** Its homebrewed mead

  ○ **D.** All of its waiters and waitresses are little people

4. What is the name of the island where the skull of a human ancestor (*Homo floresiensis*) was dubbed a "hobbit" in 2004?

  ○ **A.** Flores

  ○ **B.** Madagascar

  ○ **C.** Nihoa (Hawaii)

  ○ **D.** Galapagos

the hoard

Greed and a lust for physical objects is a theme that runs through more of Tolkien's work than The Hobbit *and* The Lord of the Rings. *A poem originally titled "Iumonna Gold Gadre Bewunden" and later renamed "The Hoard" is the tale of a hoard of riches passed down from owner to owner, all of whom meet terrible ends, cursed by the very thing that (in most cases) drove them to wealth and power. Even elves and dragons succumb. Tolkien later assigned authorship of the poem to Bilbo, even though the poem predated the creation of Bilbo by several years.*

5. What company developed a microprocessor codenamed "The Hobbit" in the early 1990s?

_____

6. In what country was a commemorative *The Hobbit* stamp made in 1998?

_____

7. When Bilbo finds Sting, two other ancient swords are found. What are their names and who obtains them?

_____

8. Durin's Day is the name of the dwarves' New Year.

○ **A.** True.

○ **B.** False.

9. Dwarf women, like dwarf men, have beards.

    ○ **A.** True.

    ○ **B.** False.

10. Which of the following is *not* a name of one of the Seven Ancestors of Dwarves?

    ○ **A.** Longbeards

    ○ **B.** Steelfists

    ○ **C.** Blacklocks

    ○ **D.** Stonefoots

11. How many runes are there in the rune alphabet?

_____

12. What was the name of the ancient elf who developed the rune alphabet, later adopted and propagated by the dwarves?

_____

13. What is the elvish (and therefore proper) name of the rune alphabet?

_____

14. What is the name of the book Meriadoc Brandybuck wrote about the histories and qualities of the Shire's pipe-weed?

_____

The Silmarilli

*The namesake of Tolkien's core mythology (*The Silmarillion*), the silmarilli (or silmaril, singular) were three jewels created by the Children of Ilúvatar. The jewels shine like the Two Trees of Valinor. They are at once a source of pride and beauty as well as lust, greed, and quarreling. One became the indirect source of light contained in the Phial of Galadriel. Some theorize that the Arkenstone is in fact one of the lost silmarilli, though that is unlikely. The true silmarilli would burn and wither any impure hand that touched them.*

15. Golfimbul, the goblin king killed by the Bullroarer, was originally named Fingolfin, but Tolkien changed the name because Fingolfin was already the name of a renowned dwarf king in *The Silmarillion*.

    ○ **A.** True.

    ○ **B.** False.

16. Though it is decidedly different from our own, Tolkien fully intends for Middle-earth to be the ancient and forgotten world of our own planet, Earth.

    ○ **A.** True.

    ○ **B.** False.

17. One can assume that Bilbo once looked up at the same constellations that we see, because Frodo notices this constellation in *The Fellowship of the Ring*, which Tolkien calls the "Sickle." What do we call it?

_____

18. According to *The Book of Lost Tales*, in Middle-earth lexicon the term "fairy" means "elf."

   ◯ **A.** True.

   ◯ **B.** False.

19. In the mythology of *The Silmarillion*, dwarves were good-natured, but seldom seen or heard from (perhaps owing to *The Silmarillion* being an elvish history).

   ◯ **A.** True.

   ◯ **B.** False.

20. In Middle-earth mythology, the word "gnome" is seldom used, but it does occur. To what group of people does it refer?

_____

21. Tolkien once stated in an interview that the dwarves bore many similarities to, and were at least partially inspired by, this religious group of people.

_____

22. The first orcs were in fact elves, carried off by Morgoth from the Awakening Place and corrupted.

   ◯ **A.** True.

   ◯ **B.** False.

the aFterLIFe

If you're a resident of Middle-earth, what happens to you when you die seems to depend largely on your race. When men die, their souls leave Creation, never to return. When elves die, they travel to the Halls of Mandos in Valinor, their souls bound to the fate of Middle-earth. The fate of dwarves is a bit murky. Elves long maintained that dwarves had no souls, and at best returned to the earth from which they were created. But it is also said that Aulë, an Aratar, cared for them and allows their souls to return to him in Valinor.

23. Glamdring, it is later revealed, once belonged to Lord Elrond himself, who identifies the sword for Gandalf.

⭘ **A.** True.

⭘ **B.** False.

24. Due to difficulties of astral calculation and prediction, the dwarves are uncertain of when their calendar's New Year takes place.

⭘ **A.** True.

⭘ **B.** False.

25. Other than Bilbo, and Samwise (possibly), name another character in Tolkien lore considered a spider-slayer.

_____

26. In *The Silmarillion*, Tolkien provides an entire tale of the creation of the Sun and the Moon. From what direction do they rise in Middle-earth?

_____

27. The elves are so adept at linguistics—indeed, they taught language to the other free peoples of Middle-earth—that they called themselves by this name, which in Elvish literally means "the speakers."

28. Aside from dwarves and elves, few of the inhabitants of Middle-earth have heard of hobbits. What people, who play an important part in *The Lord of the Rings*, have heard tales of the halfling folk who live in holes in sand dunes?

The speech of middle earth

Tolkien began to invent languages when he was quite young, and he tinkered with those of Middle-earth practically until the time of his death.

He seems to have made an attempt to reflect the social status as well as the character of various figures in their speech—for instance, all the hobbits speak in what we would consider a normal, everyday idiom. So do the dwarves, when Bilbo first meets them, but by the end of the story, at times their speech increases in seriousness and heroic structure. When Dain and his troops confront Bard at the Lonely Mountain, the dwarf asks, "But who are you who sit in the plain as foes before defended walls?" This, as Tolkien is helpful enough to tell us, is "the polite and rather old-fashioned language of such occasions."

Bilbo, of course, is notable for his down-to-Middle-earth sensibility, and when he speaks it's in short, clear sentences. If we assume that The Lord of the Rings was jointly written, in the form of The Red Book of Westmarch, by Bilbo and Frodo, we can guess that the straightforward and occasionally simple language of the early chapters reflects Bilbo's contribution, while the language grows more solemn and epic as Frodo takes over the writing.

29. There are only two instances of an elf becoming intoxicated in Tolkien's works. Once, in the cellar of the Wood-elves' cave in *The Hobbit*. What is the name of the other tale with a drunken elf?

_____

30. Deep-elves are known as such because they tend to live underground (as the elves in Mirkwood do).

○ **A.** True.

○ **B.** False.

31. Other than the Mayor of the Shire, the Master of Lake-town is the only politician (or elected official) ever mentioned in Middle-earth.

○ **A.** True.

○ **B.** False.

32. Though not all take place in Middle-earth, dragons are a recurring presence in Tolkien's stories. Match the Tolkien hero to his dragon nemesis:

A. Túrin   **i.** Smaug

B. Bilbo   **ii.** Ancalagon the Black

C. Giles   **iii.** Glaurung

D. Roverandom   **iv.** Chrysophylax

E. The Host of Valinor   **v.** Great White Dragon

33. Of all of the famed dragons in Tolkien's mythology, only one is notably wingless. Which dragon is it?

_____

34. According to Tolkien, Frodo fails at his mission to destroy the One Ring.

○ **A.** True.

○ **B.** False.

35. In *The Lord of the Rings*, when Elrond refers to the Last Alliance, he is referring to the Battle of Five Armies.

○ **A.** True.

○ **B.** False.

36. What is the Middle-earth term for the "disease" that infects people who lust after gold and other treasures?

_____

37. In *The Hobbit*, Bilbo describes eating *cram*, a type of bread. In *The Lord of the Rings*, Frodo and his companions eat *lembas*. What is the difference between *cram* and *lembas*?

_____

38. The three Elven Rings of Power, one possessed by Lord Elrond, represent three different elements. What are they?

_____

39. Which of the rings from Question 38 was held by Elrond?

_____

40. The Seven Fathers of the Dwarves are said to have awoken in the mountains, from the rocks themselves. What is the name of the mountain where Thorin's great ancestor, Durin, awoke?

_____

41. Dwarves are said to propagate very slowly. What is the primary reason?

○ **A.** A dwarf may only reproduce once in his lifetime

○ **B.** There is always the same number of dwarves, and they live very long lives

○ **C.** There are very few dwarf women

○ **D.** Most dwarves die as babies, before they are matured

42. According to _The Hobbit_, hobbits are still alive today but are rare and hidden away from modern man.

○ **A.** True.

○ **B.** False.

43. As a boy under Elrond's care, Aragorn went by a different name to hide his identity from Sauron. What was it?

_____

Lake-town as a Fortress

It may seem pretty obvious to us, knowing that Smaug is sleeping under the Mountain, ready to raid Lake-town any time he fancies, that the defenses of the men of Dale are pitifully inadequate. However, against an attack by orcs or other land-confined creatures, they were pretty well defended.

Tolkien was well acquainted with the archaeological finds in Switzerland and elsewhere of ancient towns built on pilings in the middle of lakes. In fact, the remains of a lake town were found not far from Tolkien's home at the time he was writing The Hobbit, in Glastonbury.

Such a situation gave the towns a permanent moat, as well as a ready source of water both for drinking and to extinguish flames in the event of a fire attack. Lake-town, depicted by Tolkien in one of his drawings, could be reached by a long, wooden bridge that could easily be destroyed in the event of an attack and rebuilt after the besiegers had moved on.

All of this makes sense when you consider that Esgaroth and the Lonely Mountain aren't that far (relatively) from the Grey Mountains, which, as Gandalf warned the hobbit, were "simply stiff with goblins, hobgoblins, and orcs of the worst description."

44. Virtually all of the living creatures of Middle-earth are created by a god or spirit of Valinor. What god creates the eagles?

_____

45. Though he hates to travel and is rarely seen, Radagast is to animals what Gandalf is to the free people of Middle-earth.

○ **A.** True.

○ **B.** False.

46. Which Aratar, who also created the Two Lamps of Valar, the vessels of the Sun and Moon, created the dwarves?

47. In what city does Gandalf recall the events of *The Hobbit* for Frodo, Sam, Merry, Pippin, and Gimli, according to *The Quest of Erebor*?

48. The elvish solar year begins with a day called *yestarë*, which is the day before the first full day of summer.

    ○ **A.** True.

    ○ **B.** False.

49. Into how many books is *The Lord of the Rings* divided?

The Council of Elrond

The meeting of the free peoples of Middle-earth to discuss the course of action in regard to the One Ring is a famous scene in Middle-earth's history, but can you name all of the attendees? Elrond, Gandalf, Glorfindel, Erestor, Gloin, Gimli, Galdor, Legolas, other counselors of the house of Elrond, Aragorn, Boromir of Gondor, Bilbo, Frodo, and Sam (though he was not invited) were all present at the meeting.

50. Gimli, the lone dwarf in the Fellowship, grew up in Erebor, the Kingdom Under the Mountain.

○ **A.** True.

○ **B.** False.

51. In Tolkien lore, what is the standard distinction between Light-elves and Dark-elves?

○ **A.** The color of their skin

○ **B.** Dark-elves live only in Mirkwood Forest

○ **C.** Dark-elves never leave Middle-earth for the West

○ **D.** Only Light-elves are allowed to take council in Rivendell

52. What is the Common translation of *mithril*?

_____

53. Which of the following languages is *not* a form of Elvish?

○ **A.** Quenya

○ **B.** Khuzdul

○ **C.** Sindarin

○ **D.** Telerin

54. Lord Elrond refers to the Goblin Wars. What is the proper name of these wars?

○ **A.** The Wars of Gondolin

○ **B.** The Wars of Glorfindel

○ **C.** The Wars of Beleriand

○ **D.** The Wars of Illuin

55. What is a female elf called in the Common tongue?

_____

56. Match the race to the number of Rings of Power they were given:

A. Men	**i.** 3
B. Elves	**ii.** 7
C. Dwarves	**iii.** 9
D. Hobbits	**iv.** 0

57. Though it is published as a single volume, how many parts comprise *The Silmarillion*?

_____

58. *The Silmarillion* was originally intended to be a mythology that would explain South African history and culture.

○ **A.** True.

○ **B.** False.

59. What is the title of the first story Tolkien wrote for *The Silmarillion*, completed in 1916 after he returned home from France in World War I?

_____

60. Though by sticking to the road, Bilbo and his companions miss it on their way to Rivendell, what is the name of the ancient watchtower where Frodo is stabbed by a Morgul blade?

_____

RIDDLE ME A RIDDLE

A number of readers asked Tolkien (and subsequent critics and researchers have asked themselves) where the author got the riddles he used in the contest between Gollum and Bilbo.

The tradition of riddling games is very old, and Tolkien was familiar with them from the Icelandic Eddas that he and the Coalbiters had read 'round the stove in winter. Riddles go back to Classical literature as well; Oedipus becomes the ruler of Thebes after successfully solving the riddle posed by the Sphinx.

According to Tolkien, he made all of them up except for "Thirty white horses on a red hill" and "No-legs." Both of these were traditional nursery riddles that Tolkien remembered from his own youth.

Riddles are interesting as well for what they tell us about Gollum. Gandalf, in The Fellowship of the Ring, mentions them as some evidence that Gollum came originally from a people related to hobbits. Evidently, hobbits enjoyed riddle games; there's no mention in Lord of the Rings of any of the other peoples of Middle-earth being much interested in them. Still, the tradition has some power, because "even wicked creatures were afraid to cheat when they played at it."

61. The first published reference to Middle-earth is in the prologue of *The Lord of the Rings*.

○ **A.** True.

○ **B.** False.

62. In Tolkien's mythology, the Moon revolves around the Earth and the Earth revolves around the Sun, as it does for us.

○ **A.** True.

○ **B.** False.

63. From the Second Age to the beginning of the Third Age, the world is changed from a flat one to a round one.

○ **A.** True.

○ **B.** False.

64. What is the name of God in Middle-earth?

_____

65. Author C.S. Lewis wrote a trilogy in which his Earth was called "Middle-earth," in honor of Tolkien's still then largely unpublished works. What is the name of that trilogy?

_____

66. This entrance into Khazad-dûm and the mines of Moria temporarily stumps Gandalf in *The Fellowship of the Ring* and is named after a great dwarf lord. What is it called?

_____

A SUITABLE SUCCESSOR

A recurring theme or device in Tolkien's tales is that of the superior successor—that is, an heir or a replacement who is stronger or more capable than the one who came before, able to vanquish demons his predecessor could not. In The Hobbit, *Dain Ironfoot takes the throne Under the Mountain, replacing Thorin, who succumbed to his wounds after the Battle of Five Armies. In* The Lord of the Rings, *this continues: Frodo replaces Bilbo; Aragorn replaces Isildur; Faramir replaces his elder brother, Boromir; Gandalf supplants Saruman; even the Dark Lord himself is replacing the darkness originally provided by his master, Morgoth.*

67. Rivendell was founded by Elrond in 1697 of the Second Age. What land was he fleeing from in the wake of its destruction during the War of the Elves and Sauron?

_____

68. What is the name of the volcano where Sauron forged the One Ring, also called Mount Doom by men?

_____

69. Though the region where *The Hobbit* takes place is often referred to as "the North," there is a region still farther north, sparsely populated, called the Northern Waste.

○ **A.** True.

○ **B.** False.

70. *Mithril*, the prized metal of the dwarves and the rarest and strongest metal in Middle-earth, could only be found in the mines of Moria.

○ **A.** True.

○ **B.** False.

71. Who fashioned the Silmarils, the jewels that are at the heart of Tolkien's early mythology of Middle-earth?

_____

72. Not all men in Middle-earth are elf-friends and opposed to the Dark Lord. What are the men who rode oliphaunts into the Battle of the Pelennor Fields during the siege of Minas Tirith called?

_____

73. Though they were not warmly regarded by its residents, the Shire and its surrounding lands were protected by roaming tribes of Deep-elves.

○ **A.** True.

○ **B.** False.

74. Despite the presence of the Witch-King of Angmar, and of wizards, there are no known witches in Middle-earth.

○ **A.** True.

○ **B.** False.

MIDDLE EUROPE

Though Tolkien acknowledges that the landscape of Middle-earth was composed "dramatically, rather than geologically, or paleontologically," he stated repeatedly throughout his lifetime that Middle-earth was meant to be a mythology of our own Earth. He also acknowledged that the landscape had changed a great deal since the time of his stories but once indicated that he intended Hobbiton and Rivendell to be about where Oxford currently sits. By Tolkien's calculation, this puts Minas Tirith in Florence.

75. What is the famous translation of the inscription on the One Ring, revealed only by flame? The text on the ring reads: *Ash nazg durbatulûk, ash nazg gimbatul, ash nazg thrakatulûk, agh burzum-ishi krimpatul.*

_____

76. Saradoc Brandybuck, Master of Buckland and father of Meriadoc Brandybuck, owned and operated the Green Dragon Inn.

○ **A.** True.

○ **B.** False.

77. The first day of a new year on the Shire Calendar always falls on the first day of the week, and a year always ends on the last day of the week. What are the first and last days of the week according to the Shire Calendar?

_____

the ORIGIN OF hobbits

Each race and nearly every species in Middle-earth has a complex and detailed history in Tolkien's mythos, except for the hobbits. Their "halfling" nickname implies that they are an offshoot of the race of men, but when or how they diverged is unknown. The first appearance of the hobbits is in the beginning of the Third Age in the vales of the upper Anduin. However, most of Tolkien's histories are from the perspective of the elves, who easily could have overlooked such small and peaceful creatures. Their relative anonymity makes their contributions to the War of the Ring even more remarkable.

78. Of the four Hobbits in the Fellowship, who was the oldest?

○ **A.** Sam

○ **B.** Frodo

○ **C.** Merry

○ **D.** Pippin

79. Where did Saruman tell Gandalf the One Ring had gone in order to quiet the Grey Wizard's suspicions about Bilbo's ring?

_____

80. According to *The Silmarillion*, Arda and Middle-earth were created by the music of spirits called the Ainur.

○ **A.** True.

○ **B.** False.

81. Put the following races into the order in which they were created: dwarves, elves, men.

_____

82. Match the race or being with the proper ratio of Elrond's blood:

A. Man   i. 4/16

B. Sindar   ii. 5/16

C. Ñoldor   iii. 1/16

D. Maiar   iv. 6/16

83. According to the elvish calendar, what day is the equivalent of their New Year (on our own calendar)?

_____

84. We use a decimal counting system, which is a base-10 counting system. What system do the elves use?

_____

85. The elves write their numbers right to left (though still typically write letters left to right).

○ **A.** True.

○ **B.** False.

the shadow realm

In addition to the perceivable physical realm of Middle-earth, there is also a "shadow realm" that exists in parallel. The shadow realm is not quite a spiritual plane, but within it oftentimes things—dark things in particular—reveal their true nature. This accounts for Frodo's ethereal visions when he wears the ring, as well as the changed appearance of the Nazgûl when they attack him at Weathertop. High elves live in and perceive both worlds simultaneously.

86. Though they stay in hiding until Sauron commands them to come forth, at least three Nazgûl, or Ringwraiths, are sent to this foul location ten years after Sauron abandons it.

_____

87. The names for much of the setting of *The Hobbit* (and other stories set in Middle-earth) were derived by Tolkien from the Norse *Edda*, or sagas. For instance, what mountain chain was named from the poem "Skírnismál"?

_____

88. What is regarded as "the lucky number" in Middle-earth?

_____

89. Who compiled *The Red Book of Westmarch*, a fictional manuscript that gives an account of the source of *The Lord of the Rings*?

_____

NAMING ThE ÑOLDOR

Naming can get confusing in Middle-earth. In addition to the myriad languages spoken and exchanged, places and people were often known by several names. Among the Ñoldor, for example, the elves receive three or more names throughout their lifetime. The first is their father-name, given by their father just after birth; typically a male elf is named after the father. Next is the mother-name, given by their mother, typically describing the nature of the child. Then, only after the elf-child has learned to use the language, is she or he allowed to name themselves. This is known as the chosen name.

90. What original document was the basis for *The Red Book of Westmarch*?

_____

91. In what three locations were the main collections of hobbit records kept?

_____

Chapter 8 Answer Key

1.	LEGO.	27.	Quendi.
2.	B.	28.	The Rohirrim.
3.	A.	29.	*The Lay of the Children of Húrin*.
4.	A.	30.	False. "Deep" refers to the depth of their knowledge.
5.	AT&T.	31.	True. He was elected by the town's "old and wise."
6.	Great Britain.		
7.	Glamdring and Orcrist by Gandalf and Thorin, respectively.	32.	A-iii, B-i, C-iv, D-v, E-ii.
		33.	Glaurung.
8.	True.	34.	True. Though he is still regarded as a hero for putting the ring in a position to be destroyed.
9.	True.		
10.	B.	35.	False.
11.	Thirty-two.	36.	Dragon sickness.
12.	Daeron of Doriath.	37.	*Cram* is made by men; *lembas* is made by elves.
13.	The Cirth.		
14.	*Herblore of the Shire*.	38.	Air, Water, and Fire.
15.	False. Fingolfin was a renowned elvish king.	39.	Air.
		40.	Mount Gundabad.
16.	True.	41.	C.
17.	The Big Dipper.	42.	True.
18.	True.	43.	Estel, which means "hope" in Elvish.
19.	False. They are often portrayed as evil beings—goblin allies and mercenaries.	44.	Manwë.
		45.	True.
20.	Deep-elves.	46.	Aulë.
21.	Jews.	47.	Minas Tirith.
22.	True.	48.	False. It begins with the first full day before spring.
23.	False. But it did at one time belong to Elrond's great-grandfather.		
		49.	Six.
24.	True.	50.	True.
25.	Beren or Eärendil.	51.	C.
26.	From the east.	52.	Grey glitter.

53.	B.
54.	C.
55.	Elf-maiden.
56.	A-iii, B-i, C-ii, D-iv.
57.	Five.
58.	False. It was meant to be a mythology of English history and culture.
59.	*The Fall of Gondolin.*
60.	The Tower of Amon Sûl.
61.	True.
62.	False. The Sun and Moon revolve around the Earth, known as Arda.
63.	False. It was the end of the First Age and the beginning of the Second.
64.	Eru Ilúvatar.
65.	The Space Trilogy.
66.	The Doors of Durin.
67.	Eregion.
68.	Orodruin.
69.	True.
70.	True.
71.	Fëanor.
72.	Haradrim.
73.	False. They were protected by Rangers, such as Aragorn.
74.	True.
75.	One Ring to rule them all, One Ring to find them, One Ring to bring them all and in the darkness bind them.
76.	False. It is never said who owns or operates the Green Dragon Inn.
77.	Saturday and Friday, respectively.
78.	B.
79.	Into the sea.

80.	True.
81.	Elves, men, dwarves.
82.	A-iv, B-ii, C-i, D-iii.
83.	March 28.
84.	Duodecimal, or base-12.
85.	True.
86.	Dol Guldur.
87.	The Misty Mountains.
88.	Fourteen.
89.	The Fairbairns, Wardens of Westmarch.
90.	Bilbo's private diary.
91.	Undertowers, Great Smials, and Brandybuck Hall.

Score Your Middle-earth Memorization!

In this chapter, there are 101 possible right answers.

If you got 0–34 right, you're a Nadorhuan. And you also probably have no idea what that means.

If you got 35–65 right, you're a Dúnadan, a mortal blessed with unusually long life. Apparently you're using that extra time to apply yourself. Glad to hear it.

If you got 66–101 right, you are an elvish lord: graceful, wise, immortal, and most of all . . . obsessed with Middle-earth.

hOBBIT MISCELLANY

One doesn't simply create an entire world top to bottom without making a few mistakes. Tolkien made his fair share, though years of meticulous revisions by him and his son Christopher, as well as the watchful eye of a dedicated fan base (hey, that's you!) have helped cover most of them.

Though he wished for *The Hobbit* and *The Lord of the Rings* to be judged on their own merits, Tolkien was never quite fully satisfied with his attempts to reconcile *The Hobbit* with the much larger world he built in *Rings* afterward. Typically, when a mistake would arise, Tolkien would simply create a new tale or back story—add a new branch to a family tree—which was perfectly acceptable to him. What few discrepancies remain are typically overlooked by fans (that's you again). Peter Jackson's goal with his three-part *Hobbit* films was to finally create a definitive hobbit tale, incorporating all of Tolkien's additions and changes.

Of course, after Tolkien, there is less accounting for holes in or changes to the text. Each new adaptation and toy brings with it a renewed potential for a blooper, a blunder, or a gaffe. Can you spot them?

1. Prior to Tolkien, what was the real historical plural for "dwarf"?

○ **A.** Dwarrows

○ **B.** Dwarfs

○ **C.** Dwarves

○ **D.** Dwarf

2. According to Tolkien, the proper pluralization of "dwarf" is "dwarves."

○ **A.** True.

○ **B.** False.

3. Famed *Star Trek* actor Leonard Nimoy released a song about *The Hobbit* on his album *The Two Sides of Leonard Nimoy*. What was the name of the track?

_____

4. A year before its release, Nimoy lip-synched the song for a variety show in a segment that lives on as what many consider to be the worst music video of all time. What was the name of the variety show?

_____

5. What was the name of the dangerous woods on the borders of the Shire?

_____

WhAT CLEARING?

In the 1977 animated film, Bilbo tells the dwarves to "run back to the Wood-elf clearing" while he fights off the giant spiders. However, in the film, the dwarves had not yet come across the elves, nor had they found their clearing. As the elves capture the dwarves, Bilbo's narration states that the elves had "returned, armed for battle," even though this was the first time the elves had been seen. It seems the scene of Bilbo and the dwarves attempting to join the Wood-elves' merrymaking was a late scratch from the film.

6. Tolkien produced a third edition of *The Hobbit* in 1966 at the request of the publisher due to the appearance of unauthorized printings of *The Lord of the Rings*.

  ○ **A.** True.

  ○ **B.** False.

7. What is the name of the Southampton bar and music venue that was sued by Saul Zaentz Company (SZC), who own the licensing rights for Tolkien film adaptations, in 2012?

  ○ **A.** The Hobbit

  ○ **B.** The Shire

  ○ **C.** Bag End

  ○ **D.** Mordor

8. The novel *There and Back Again* by Pat Murphy is a retelling of *The Hobbit* in what setting?

_____

9. What were hobbits called in Pat Murphy's *There and Back Again*?

_____

10. What Kevin Smith film famously skewers Jackson's *Lord of the Rings* trilogy (in favor of the Star Wars trilogy)?

_____

11. From 1968 to 1973, Star Trek fans embarked on a letter-writing campaign to get a live-action *Lord of the Rings* film made . . . with Leonard Nimoy as Aragorn.

○ **A.** True.

○ **B.** False.

12. In the 2011 eBook *The Wobbit*, the dwarves are bankers and the titular character is an unemployed what?

_____

MAGICAL MUSICAL INSTRUMENTS

A famous early scene in the book occurs when, after settling in and settling their stomachs at Bilbo's hobbit-hole, the dwarves produce musical instruments and begin to play. Here they sing the first song in the book and Bilbo finds himself overcome with emotion. However, it is never explained what happens to those instruments, or why the dwarves would have brought them all the way to Bag End only to leave them there.

13. In 2011, PEZ released a box set of its famed candy dispensers with the heads of *Lord of the Rings* characters, including Gandalf and Gollum.

○ **A.** True.

○ **B.** False.

14. When Gandalf tells Thorin about the fate of his father, it is a surprise to the dwarf. However, he should have known much more about this tale, as two members of his party were on a quest with Thorin's father when he disappeared. Who are they?

_____

15. When Bilbo wears the ring in *The Hobbit*, he still casts a shadow. However, when Frodo wears it in *The Lord of the Rings*, he does not.

○ **A.** True.

○ **B.** False.

16. Before Tolkien had finally settled on a name, what was the working title of *The Lord of the Rings*?

_____

17. Due to a discrepancy in the history of Thorin's family line, Tolkien was forced to make a more ancient version of this dwarf. What was his (or their) name?

_____

AS HARD AS LINEN

Though mithril *is sought after for its light weight, incomparable strength, and unfailing durability, there is some confusion as to how it feels. When Bilbo gives the mail to Frodo, he says that it is "almost as supple as linen." It is seemingly almost unnoticeable when worn. However, after Frodo puts on the mail, Bilbo gives him a slap on the back and lets out a shout, telling his heir he is "too hard now to slap." It could be that* mithril, *while light, responds differently to force. It could also be that Bilbo is merely being playful.*

18. In Chapter 2 of *The Hobbit*, it is said that the party began their journey "one fine morning just before May." However, in Chapter 8, Bilbo recalls that they had "started their journey that May morning long ago." What was the actual departure date, according to *The Quest of Erebor*?

_____

19. The orcs recognize Orcrist and Glamdring in the Misty Mountains, despite the fact that the weapons' supposed owner only fought in one major battle in the Wars of Beleriand. Who was their owner?

_____

20. It is unlikely the orcs in the Misty Mountains would be able to recognize Orcrist and Glamdring because they were said to be forged two ages and many thousands of years beforehand.

○ **A.** True.

○ **B.** False.

τhε sωοκδs οf hοββιτs

Swords play an important role in Tolkien's mythology. In The Hobbit *we have two famous swords—Glamdring and Orcrist—introduced into the story, as well as Bilbo's short sword, Sting. All three of these blades are connected to the Goblin Wars and the ancient city of Gondolin.*

Similar blades come into play in Lord of the Rings. *When setting out on the quest of the Fellowship, Gandalf wears Glamdring, and later uses it in battle with the balrog on the Bridge of Khazad-dûm. Frodo, of course, wears Sting, given to him by Bilbo. But there are other famous swords in play.*

Aragon wears Andúril, the Sword that was Broken, the sword of Isildur recovered from his body after the disaster at the Gladden Fields many years previous. And the hobbits Merry and Pippin both wear swords taken from a barrow-wight on the Barrow-downs where they nearly perished—but for the timely help of Tom Bombadil.

Merry's sword is later destroyed when he stabs the Witch-king, leader of the Ringwraiths, and it is revealed that it was created by the men of the North in ages past to battle against the very Witch-king with whom Merry fought. (Pippin's sword makes it back to the Shire; presumably later in life he hung it over the mantelpiece or something.)

Swords are the only weapons important enough to have names; we never read about the axe of Dain or anything. In fact, it's never quite clear what the weapon of choice is for the dwarves. In The Lord of the Rings, *Gimli fights with an axe, but in* The Hobbit, *Thorin carries a sword and the other dwarves, for a time at least, have bows and arrows.*

21. Bilbo makes the mistake of revealing not only his name, but also the fact that he is from the Shire, to Gollum, which eventually leads Sauron's Ringwraiths to Hobbiton.

○ **A.** True.

○ **B.** False.

22. Even though it is later established that all elvish blades glow blue in the presence of orcs, only two of the three elvish blades found in *The Hobbit* ever glow. Which one does not?

_____

23. Gandalf's staff in the first film of the three-part *The Hobbit* looks different from the staff that he has in *The Fellowship of the Ring*.

○ **A.** True.

○ **B.** False.

24. After Thorin's passing, we are told that "it was a very long time before [Bilbo] had the heart to make a joke again." But he soon spends a "warm and merry" Yuletide in a familiar place. Where is he?

_____

25. All but one actor in the Fellowship from *The Fellowship of the Ring* got the same tattoo of an Elvish character after the production. What does the character stand for?

_____

26. Which actor did not get the tattoo?

_____

The TALE OF YEARS

It's always helpful to take a quick stroll through the appendices Tolkien included in The Lord of the Rings. In them, you'll find a great deal of information about hobbits and other peoples of Middle-earth. In Appendix B, the inquisitive reader can also find out more on what various important figures in The Lord of the Rings were doing while Bilbo and the dwarves were off on the quest of Erebor. For instance:

- Aragorn, Isildur's heir, was ten years old when Bilbo and the dwarves visited Rivendell.
- Arwen, later beloved by Aragorn, was off with Galadriel in Lothlórien; she was a mere 2,680 years older than her future husband.
- Théoden of Rohan hadn't yet been born; he came into the world seven years after Bilbo returned from the Lonely Mountain.

Thirteen years after Bilbo's adventures, Mount Doom burst into flame, a sign that Sauron had, indeed, returned to his ancient stronghold in Mordor. Two years later, Aragorn met Gandalf and formed a close friendship with the old wizard. A dozen years later, a baby was born in the Shire named Frodo Baggins.

And so the pieces were on the board, and the events of The Lord of the Rings were ready to begin.

27. There is a *Lord of the Rings* tarot deck.

○ **A.** True.

○ **B.** False.

28. Led Zeppelin wrote and recorded a song partially inspired by Tolkien's work. What was it called?

_____

29. Mattel produced a line of shorter, "wider" fashion dolls in 2008, which they called "hobbit bodies."

○ **A.** True.

○ **B.** False.

30. What automaker produced a moped called the "Hobbit," along with print advertisements made complete with creepy, scarecrow, Rumpelstiltskin renditions of hobbits?

_____

31. Bilbo is struck in the head by a rock during the Battle of Five Armies. What keeps him alive?

_____

32. The moon-runes on the map read in part, "Stand by the grey stone when the thrush knocks." However, for most early printings of the book, Lord Elrond reads this incorrectly by a single word. How does he read it?

_____

hobbit holes

In 2012, Etsy.com seller Wooden Wonders began producing and selling "Hobbit Holes" for about $3,000 apiece. Marketed as playhouses for children, outdoor work stations, or chicken coops, the holes amount to oddly shaped toolsheds. Still, they come with the trademark circular door and colorful trim you would expect to see in the Shire. Buying one might be the closest you ever come to living in a hobbit-hole.

33. The calendar used in *The Hobbit* must be Gregorian based on the correspondence of dates with the moon cycles.

○ **A.** True.

○ **B.** False.

34. When he wrote *The Hobbit*, Tolkien had not yet invented the Shire Calendar (it's found in Appendix D of *The Lord of the Rings*) and therefore couldn't convert the timeline of *The Hobbit* over to the hobbits' calendar.

○ **A.** True.

○ **B.** False.

35. The precise date of Bilbo's birthday is nowhere mentioned in *The Hobbit*—however, after assigning one in the prologue to *The Lord of the Rings*, his birthday suddenly coincided with what key event in Bilbo's tale?

_____

36. Gollum often sneaks up on orcs if he is in need of a meal . . . but what makes his "sneaking" unlikely, based on his description in the text?

_____

37. What language did not get a translation of *The Hobbit* until March 2012—with an initial print run of just eighteen copies?

_____

Luck versus Fate

An underlying theme in both The Hobbit *and* The Lord of the Rings *is the role of chance versus the role of fate. Tolkien brings this up for the first time in the important scene when Bilbo finds the ring. Bilbo, groping in the dark of the goblin tunnels, finds the ring lying on the ground. "It was a turning point in his career, but he did not know it."*

Certainly he thinks it's a very fortunate chance, enabling him to escape Gollum and the goblins guarding the exit from the tunnels.

Later, when he begins to use the ring regularly, he still thinks of it in terms of luck. "Perhaps I have begun to trust to my luck more than I used to in the old days," he tells the dwarves.

When Bilbo, triumphant after his many adventures, comes home, he still thinks of himself as essentially lucky. He was, after all, "chosen for the lucky number" (as he tells Smaug). And he is apparently blessed with great wealth, long life, and complete happiness.

Except . . .

Well, of course, except for the ring. And, as Gandalf explains to Frodo at the beginning of his adventures, there was nothing "lucky" about Bilbo finding the ring. It was all part of a greater cosmic plan, the details of which are hidden from mortals. "I can put it no plainer than by saying that Bilbo was meant *to find the Ring and* not *by its maker."*

Tolkien, later in life, began a revision of The Hobbit *to make its tone and handling of certain matters fit better with* The Lord of the Rings. *Sadly, he ceased the project before reaching Bilbo's encounter with Gollum. It's interesting to think of what he might have said about fate and luck in revising that scene.*

38. In 1966, when Bill Snyder realized that, in order to retain the film rights to *The Hobbit*, he could make a film of any length or quality . . . how quickly was the film made?

39. Tolkien was often seen smoking from a long pipe. As he probably couldn't get his hands on any Longbottom Leaf, what was his tobacco brand of choice?

_____

40. What is the official toast to the late, great J.R.R. Tolkien?

_____

Chapter 9 Answer Key

1.	A.	21.	True.
2.	False, though he uses it "accidentally" repeatedly throughout the text and it stuck.	22.	Orcrist.
		23.	True.
3.	"The Ballad of Bilbo Baggins."	24.	Beorn's house.
4.	Malibu U.	25.	Nine—the number of individuals in the Fellowship.
5.	The Old Forest.	26.	John Rhys-Davies.
6.	True.	27.	True.
7.	A.	28.	"Battle of Evermore."
8.	Space.	29.	False. Though the dolls do exist, the term "hobbit bodies" was coined by bloggers, not actually used by the doll manufacturer.
9.	Norbits.		
10.	*Clerks II.*	30.	Honda.
11.	True.	31.	A helmet, though the text had never described a helmet on Bilbo before.
12.	Bank teller.	32.	"Stand by the grey stone *where* the thrush knocks."
13.	True.	33.	False. In truth, neither calendar lines up correctly with the known moon cycle.
14.	Balin and Dwalin.		
15.	True.	34.	True.
16.	"The New Hobbit" or "The Magic Ring."	35.	The Unexpected Party's arrival at Lake-town.
17.	Thráin.	36.	His eyes glow in the dark.
18.	April 27.	37.	Irish.
19.	King Turgon.	38.	In about a month.
20.	True.	39.	Navy Cut.
		40.	"The Professor."

Score Your Miscellany Wisdom!

In this section, there are 40 possible right answers.

If you got 0–14 right, you see the world through rose-colored glasses. You can't seem to find the mistakes!

If you got 15–30 right, you're a descendant of dragons. Wise, clever, and good at spotting mistakes. But you're not without your weak spots . . .

If you got 31–40 right, you're a Took. Brash, fool-hearty, and brave. You've got a knack for causing bloopers and getting into blunders—as well as out of them.

FAN SCORECARD

The time has finally come for you to take your place in Middle-earth's history. Flip back to the end of each chapter and check the answer key, then write down your totals here for easy reference. Add them up and see where you stand on the spectrum of True Hobbit Fandom.

_____ **CHAPTER 1** (100 possible points)

_____ **CHAPTER 2** (97 possible points)

_____ **CHAPTER 3** (95 possible points)

_____ **CHAPTER 4** (98 possible points)

_____ **CHAPTER 5** (92 possible points)

_____ **CHAPTER 6** (99 possible points)

_____ **CHAPTER 7** (103 possible points)

_____ **CHAPTER 8** (101 possible points)

_____ **CHAPTER 9** (40 possible points)

_____ **TOTAL** (825 possible points)

If you . . .

- **scored 776 to 825**, you're an **Expert**! There are few who could ever challenge your knowledge of Arda—even the Tolkiens. If there are ever any apocalypse-harbinger-mind-control rings that need destroying, you're the first one we'll call.

- **scored 726 to 775**, you're a **Connoisseur**! The next time you're at a loss for a Halloween costume, consider going as a hobbit. All you have to worry about is the look—you've got the mind part down.

- **scored 626 to 725**, you're a **True Fan**! Any trivia team, or rag-tag party of adventurers, would be lucky to have you. You possess the keen ability to fell *Hobbit*-related questions like a Ranger to an orc.

- **scored 500 to 625**, you're a **Buff**! Even if you occasionally have difficulty distinguishing male dwarves from female dwarves, your mind is as broad as a battle-axe and as powerful as an elvish bow.

- **scored less than 500**, you're an **Enthusiast**! So maybe you're not quite a wizard yet. The good news is you have an entire library of books, games, radio shows, and movies to dig through before you've exhausted your "Mind of Moria."

INDEX

Page numbers of entries that appear in questions are bold, while those in the sidebars are not.